TONS of Things to Do for HAWAI'I'S KIDS

Activities, Adventures & Excursions for Keiki Eager to Explore

TONS of Things to Do for HAWAI'I'S KIDS

**Activities, Adventures & Excursions
for Keiki Eager to Explore**

O'AHU

Carrie Ching

Illustrated by
Lance Bowen

BEACHHOUSE
PUBLISHING, LLC

Every effort has been made to ensure the accuracy of the material
contained in this book. Recreational activities contain elements of risk and it
is the responsibility of the reader to assess the risks and determine the appropriate
and safe action. The publisher and the author of this book disclaim any responsibility for any
injury, harm or illness that may occur to anyone through, or by use of, the information
in this book or through errors, omissions or misleading information.

Unless otherwise noted, photos by Carrie Ching, Jane Hopkins, and Ian Gillespie
Sign Hunt, Try Look!, Did You Know?, Fun Idea!, word searches,
crosswords, and design by Jane Hopkins

ISBN 0-9729905-2-6
Library of Congress Catalog Number: 2004101186

First Printing, July 2004

BeachHouse Publishing, LLC
PO Box 2926
'Ewa Beach, HI 96706
beachhousepub@hawaii.rr.com

Printed in Korea

TABLE OF CONTENTS

FOREWORD (FOR ADULTS)

How often have you heard that young, familiar voice complaining, "I'm bored. There's nothing to do."? And in response, your brain skips through all the chores that need to be done and all the errands that need to be run. You sigh, unable to answer, only to find your children sitting in front of the TV or the computer.

This book is meant to be an idea book for kids and adults to use together. It will save you on the days when the idea box in your head is empty. It's a reminder of all the wonderful things O'ahu has to offer. From playing with clay and creating sculptures at the Contemporary Museum's Art Spree, to hiking up to Mānoa Falls (something you always meant to do), to exploring a botanic garden on the other side of the island, to taking taiko drumming lessons—*Tons of Things to Do for Hawai'i's Kids* offers so many ideas summer won't be long enough to do them all.

Every chapter is so jam packed with great island fun that if you don't have a kid, you'll want to borrow one. There are pages and pages of adventures giving you the urge to get out and do them all. You'll find dozens of things you didn't even know about, and dozens more you haven't done since your own small-kid days.

How lucky we are that our city ends at a beach, our air is clear, and our water clean. What this well-crafted, kid-friendly guide book tells us is that, by just about any measure, Hawai'i has more free things to do than any other state. There are not only a number of activities outdoors, but many indoors—and all of them will teach you and your children something new.

There's something for every kid's discerning interests. Are insects your thing? Plan a day with the Hawai'i Nature Center. Love horses? Enjoy a polo game up at Mokulē'ia or Waimānalo or take riding lessons at Kualoa Ranch. Is your son the next Picasso? All the art museums on the island offer programs for kids. Love the beach, but tired of going to the same one day after day? Pack a picnic lunch and take the kids to the other side of the island—there are plenty of things to do on the ride there. The book includes car games: Sign Hunt, Try Look!, and crossword puzzles, word searches, jokes and fun facts. There's even "Fun Idea!" sidebars that will trigger your kid's imagination and creativity. Keep this book in your car and bring adventure into your day.

Safety tips and information are also included, but do your own additional research for any new adventure you embark on.

With fun illustrations by Maui artist Lance Bowen, this book is meant to be enjoyed, used and shared. Write in it, play the games, and jot down notes for your next excursion—suggested itineraries are included in the back of the book.

Bored? Never again. Grab the book, paper and a pencil and head for the car. O'ahu is just waiting to be explored.

—Lynn Cook
Freelance family writer, author,
and regular contributor to
Hawaii Parent Magazine

Aquarium After Dark features a lights-out look at the Waikīkī Aquarium's exhibits. See what happens on the reef when the sun goes down. This class for families is like night diving without getting wet! PHOTO COURTESY OF THE WAIKĪKĪ AQUARIUM

INTRODUCTION (FOR KIDS)

Hawai'i is one of the most beautiful and exciting places on Earth. Why else would more than six million people come to visit every year? On O'ahu, "the gathering place" of the Hawaiian Islands, there are beautiful beaches, lush forests, ancient volcanoes and even deserts—and no matter where you are, the exciting city of Honolulu is always nearby.

When you live on an island, sometimes you get used to swimming at the same beaches, hiking the same trails, and skateboarding in the same parks all the time. When you get bored, you end up just sitting in front of the TV or playing video games ALL DAY, even when it's warm and sunny outside! You're missing out on SO MUCH!

I bet there are hundreds of places to go and things to do on O'ahu that you've never even heard of before.

Have you ever taken a ride on the old train at 'Ewa Beach Railway? Or dangled a hundred feet above Waikīkī under a humongous kite? Have you been to the Honolulu Zoo in the moonlight to see the animals that only come out at night? Well, put down the TV remote and let's go check it out.

PUT YOURSELF ON THE MAP

Let's start out by taking a look at a map of O'ahu. Where do you live? Can you find where your school is? Where do your aunties, uncles, cousins and grandparents live? How about your best friend? Where does Mom or Dad work?

Start with this fun, old map to figure out what places and activities are near your home, and which ones are farther away. You might need to ask Mom, Dad, auntie, uncle, Tutu or big brother or sister to drive you to some of the places that are across the island. You can plan out a fun day of activities. They could probably learn a lot from this book, too.

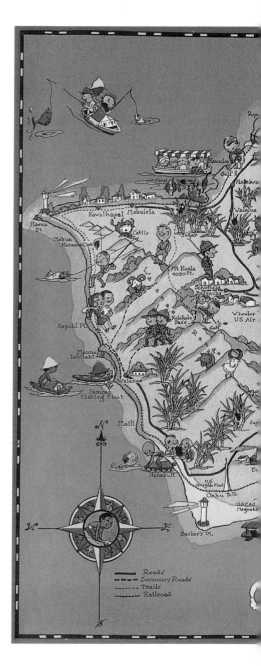

Island of Oahu

This Cartograph is lined and colored to the thrills that greeted me when I first touched the Hawaiian Islands some 2000 miles from America's western edge, .. at the "Crossroads of the Pacific." In the sun-filled corners of this island of Oahu you'll find, as I did, a lifetime of high adventure.

Issued by the Hawaii Tourist Bureau (of Honolulu, U.S.A.)

FUN AT THE BEACH

It's HOT outside—get yourself in the water and cool off! Maybe you've been to the beach a gazillion times before, but have you ever searched for hermit crabs at Shark's Cove, ridden the waves at Kalama Beach Park or snorkeled in Waimea Bay under the warm summer sun? Everyone has their favorite beach, but Hawai'i is so much more fun when you mix things up by going to new places. Go to a beach you've never been to before. Try a new water sport—maybe skimboarding? Or discover a new hobby—ever collected 'opihi? You can take lessons, too: from wakeboarding lessons in Hawai'i Kai to longboarding in Waikīkī, the island has much more to offer than you might think.

Good Beaches for Kids

Be adventurous and visit a new beach—here are some suggestions for safe, sunny spots on O'ahu. (All beaches on O'ahu are public.)

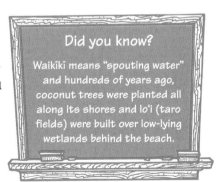

Did you know?

Waikīkī means "spouting water" and hundreds of years ago, coconut trees were planted all along its shores and lo'i (taro fields) were built over low-lying wetlands behind the beach.

SOUTH SHORE/TOWN

Waikīkī Beach

Waikīkī is actually made up of many beaches stacked side-by-side on a two-mile stretch of sand. Some of the best ones for kids are the Waikīkī Beach Center and Kūhiō Beach (where Kapahulu Avenue meets the beach) and Queen's Surf, Kapiʻolani Beach Park and San Souci (also called "Kaimana," towards Diamond Head). Safe swimming conditions and lifeguards at almost all beaches. Many beaches have food and drink stands. All along Kalākaua Avenue in Waikīkī.

Just for laughs

Why did the chicken cross the beach?

To get to the other tide.

Ala Moana Beach Park

Very popular beach and park with lifeguards, fitness stations and snack shop. Across from Ala Moana Shopping Center at 1201 Ala Moana Boulevard.

Kids shower off after a day spent at Ala Moana Beach Park.

Kahanamoku Beach and Lagoon

The public saltwater lagoon and sandy beach are located on the grounds of the Hilton Hawaiian Village. Very safe swimming, lifeguards and snack shop. 2500 Kālia Road in Waikīkī.

Queen's Pier, Waikīkī

Magic Island Beach Park and Lagoon

Popular beach next to Ala Wai Yacht Harbor. Rock retaining wall protects the calm lagoon from big waves. Lifeguards and snack shop at Ala Moana Beach Park. Located at eastern end of Ala Moana Beach Park.

Kāhala Beach

Long, narrow beach with shallow reef bottom and sandy pockets for swimming. No lifeguard or restrooms. Runs along Kāhala Avenue; six public right-of-way entrances from the road, try the one at the end of Hunakai Street.

> PARENTS: Pay attention to the seasons and wave conditions at Oʻahu's beaches. During the summer (May through August), the North Shore beaches are usually safe for swimming, while the South Shore beaches are hit by high swells. During the winter (October through April), the South Shore is usually safe, while the North Shore beaches have heavy surf and are very dangerous for swimming. Watch for warning flags at the beaches and ask a lifeguard about swimming conditions. Be cautious and use your own judgment when lifeguards aren't present. Don't let kids swim alone, and beware of heavy currents and undertow that are difficult for little ones to swim against.
>
> Also, bring "just in case" supplies with you to the beach. Sunscreen (SPF 15 or higher) should be applied at least 30 minutes before going in the water. Bring drinking water to stay hydrated in the hot sun. Pack some meat tenderizer in case of jellyfish, Portuguese man-o-war or bee stings.

Life's A Beach

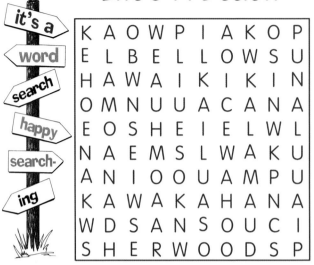

it's a
word
search
happy
search-
ing

```
K A O W P I A K O P
E L B E L L O W S U
H A W A I K I K I N
O M N U U A C A N A
E O S H E I E L W L
N A E M S L W A K U
A N I O O U A M P U
K A W A K A H A N A
W D S A N S O U C I
S H E R W O O D S P
```

Try to find all these O'ahu beaches. Some are horizontal, vertical, diagonal and backwards. Circle the ones you find.

Ala Moana   Kahana
Kāne'ohe   San Souci
Waimea   Punalu'u
Waikīkī   Sherwoods
Kalama   'Ewa
Kailua   Pōka'i

Hanauma Bay
Very popular beach and protected bay. Good snorkeling and swimming. Stay near the beach, avoid the rocky ledges on either side. Hanauma Bay is an underwater wildlife refuge: Please don't feed the fish or bother any creatures here. Parking donation of $5 per car. Near Koko Head at 7455 Kalaniana'ole Highway.

EAST SIDE
Kahana Bay
Wide, flat beach located between two former Hawaiian fishponds. Freshwater stream crosses beach at south end, boat ramp located on

Try look!

(it's a car game for kids)

While you're in the car, going to the beach, see who can find these things. Whoever finds it first gets the points.

"Live Aloha" sticker on a car bumper   **2 points**

Kamehameha Schools sticker in window   **3 points**

A kid on a bike riding with a surfboard   **5 points**

north end. Popular with fishermen. Safe swimming, good bodysurfing for beginners. Lifeguards June through August. Parking lot at 52-222 Kamehameha Highway.

Kualoa Regional Park

Grassy park and long, narrow beach with safe swimming. Occasional currents and sandy bottom with some coral. Lifeguards daily June through August and on weekends. 49-600 block of Kamehameha Highway.

Kāneʻohe Bay Sandbar

At low tide, Kāneʻohe Bay is dotted with sandbars that emerge like tiny islands. You can only get there on a private boat, but it's a great place for family picnics, frisbees and swimming on a sunny day. Very shallow waters

Keiki cool off at Lanikai Beach.

Kailua Beach is great for keiki ready to ride the waves. Photo © Douglas Peebles

on the sandbar, but the bottom drops off quickly farther out. No lifeguard or restrooms.

Kailua Beach Park
Very popular wide, sandy beach with safe swimming, picnic areas and restrooms. Avoid the brackish stream opening near south end. Lifeguards on duty. 450 Kawailoa Road.

Kalama Beach Park
Good place for boogie boarding, bodysurfing and shorebreak surfing. Restrooms and showers, but no lifeguard. Located at the 300 block of North Kalāheo Avenue in Kailua, turn into parking lot at sign.

Lanikai Beach
Narrow, sandy beach in Kailua, safe swimming in protected bay. No lifeguard, nearest public restrooms at Kailua Boat Ramp. Park on Mokulua Drive, public beach accesses between private homes.

Waimānalo Beach Park
Wide, sandy beach, occasional currents, small-to-medium shorebreak waves. No lifeguard. 41-741 Kalaniana'ole Highway.

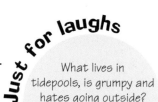
Waimānalo Bay State Recreation Area (Also "Sherwoods Forest")
Same conditions at Waimānalo Beach Park. No lifeguard. Located off Kalaniana'ole Highway across from the polo fields. Drive through the gate and follow the road to the parking lot. Access to the beach can also be found at the end of Aloiloi Street.

Bellows Beach Park
Same conditions as Waimānalo Beach Park. Public access and lifeguards only on weekends. The beach is bordered by two freshwater streams. Take turn-off from Kalaniana'ole into Bellows Field and go through gate.

NORTH SHORE

Mālaekahana Bay State Recreation Area
Sandy beach where you can sometimes find shells. On calm days, you can wade across the reef to Goat Island. No lifeguard. Off Kamehameha Highway between Lā'ie and Kahuku.

Waimea Bay
Although very dangerous during the gigantic winter surf (October through April), Waimea Bay is flat like a pond during high summer (May through August) and can be a great place to swim and snorkel. Very wide sandy beach, lifeguards year-round. 61-031 Kamehameha Highway across from Waimea Valley entrance.

Hale'iwa Beach Park
Breakwaters offshore keep the inshore area safe for swimming all year. Lifeguards daily during the summer. 62-449 Kamehameha Highway.

Safety First!

Swimming and playing at the beach with family and friends is a great way to spend the day. But parents, keep those keiki safe!

No matter what your child's age, always keep an eye out when at the beach—especially watch those 7 and under.

Sun safety
- Limit sun exposure during times of the day when the sun's rays are the strongest—usually between 10 AM and 4 PM. Many of Hawai'i's beaches have shaded areas.
- Make sure your keiki wear sunglasses and/or hats, especially the young ones.
- Generously apply sunscreens that block UVA and UVB rays. The Sun Protective Factor (SPF) should be at least 15. And don't be fooled if it's cloudy. Your child can still get sunburned. Make sure you use a waterproof sunscreen and reapply every few hours.
- Have water on hand and make sure your keiki keep hydrated. Sodas and juices won't do—water is the best.

Beach safety
- The best thing anyone can do is teach their keiki how to swim.
- Regardless of age and experience, all keiki need to be carefully watched when they are by water of any kind.
- Don't assume the inflatable toy or raft your keiki is swimming with is a good substitute for careful supervision. A wave can easily make that child slip off.
- Stay within designated swimming areas—especially at beaches that also cater to kayakers, windsurfers and small ocean craft.
- If there's a lifeguard, stay within his/her sightline.
- NEVER let your keiki swim alone.
- Check surf conditions BEFORE you enter the water.
- Watch for signs at the beach alerting people of hazardous conditions.
- Keep a lookout for aquatic life. Teach your children to leave water plants and animals alone. You never know when one might be dangerous.
- Parents should learn CPR. Contact your local Red Cross chapter for information on courses.

(For additional information, check the American Red Cross website at www.redcross.org).

Tidepools

it's a
word
search
happy
search-
ing

Try to find all these creatures in the tidepool. Some are horizontal, vertical, diagonal and backwards. Circle the ones you find.

shells

sea urchin

rocks

seaweed

starfish

hermit crab

fish

coral

crabs

WEST SIDE

Pōka'i Bay Beach Park (Also Nene'u Beach)

The most protected beach on the Wai'anae coastline. Shallow, safe swimming, but watch out for boat traffic! Lifeguard during the summer and on weekends. 85-037 Wai'anae Valley Road.

Fun Things to Do at the Beach

On your next trip to the beach, get creative and try something new. Be a scientist and discoverer. The beach is

Viewing Box

To make a simple viewing box you can use to see all the creatures hiding and swimming in tide pools, take a plastic milk or juice jug and cut off the bottom (have an adult help). Cover the bottom of the jug with clear, thick plastic and cut down to size. Using duct tape, attach the plastic to the bottom. Wrap it well so it doesn't fall off in the water or let water in. At the edge of the tidepool, put the jug in the water and look through the spout. You'll get a close and clear look at the creatures underwater—without disturbing their home.

not just a great place to get a suntan—it's full of life and wonder. From tidepooling to snorkeling to beachcombing, you can see incredible living organisms—some found no place else on earth.

Tidepooling

Take a camera, a viewing box (see above) and some friends and check out a local tidepool. You can find little fish, hermit crabs, snails, starfish, seaweed and lots of other living creatures. Try these favorite local tidepools. But remember, many of our reefs are protected so be careful where you walk. And don't disturb the creatures: would you want to be lifted out of your home? Check the Hawai'i DLNR website for information on how to check out tidepools safely. www.hawaii.gov/dlnr

LIFEGUARD ON DUTY

Kaʻalāwai Beach (Also "Cromwell's" or "Kaiko's" [Kaikoʻo])
Large protected tidepool on the east end of the beach near Black Point. Also,

Searching for sea creatures at the Makapuʻu tidepools.

try wading around the shallow reef along the beach. No lifeguard. From Kāhala Avenue, turn makai onto Kulamanu Place. Public access at the end of Kulamanu St.

Makapuʻu Beach Park
The ocean here is rough, only for expert bodysurfers, but there are some tidepools past the north end of the beach (near Sea Life Park). Don't get too close to the crashing waves past the rocks. Daily lifeguards. In Waimānalo at 41-095 Kalanianaʻole Highway.

Pūpūkea Beach Park (Also "Shark's Cove")
The large tidepool is protected from the waves by a high coral shelf. Calm during the summer months (very dangerous from October through April). Don't try to climb on the coral shelf as waves are known to break overhead, causing climbers to fall and be cut by the sharp coral. The

Families can explore tidepools and reef shallows with Waikīkī Aquarium naturalists. During spring and summer months, fieldtrips take place during the best daytime low tides; in fall and winter, explorations take place at night! M. PICKETT/WAIKĪKĪ AQUARIUM

large pool is often used by snorkelers and beginning scuba divers. Smaller tidepools nearby are good for wading. No lifeguard. Located on the North Shore at 59-727 Kamehameha Highway across from the Pūpūkea Foodland.

'Ewa Beach Park
Not exactly tidepools, but known all across the island as a place to collect limu or seaweed. Not good for swimming and no lifeguard. 91-027 Fort Weaver Road in 'Ewa.

Snorkeling

Put on a mask and snorkel and sink into the amazing world under the sea. You might see rainbow-colored parrotfish, little yellow-striped butterfly fish, sea cucumbers,

Safety First!

Snorkeling is a fun activity for the whole family. Keiki can discover a new world under the sea. Hawai'i's waters contain some of the most beautiful and diverse sealife around. So have fun and be careful!

Snorkeling safety
- Have your keiki practice in shallow water before venturing out deeper. For younger keiki, have them practice breathing through the snorkel while on shore.
- Make sure the face mask and snorkel are functioning properly and have no leaks.
- Keiki should learn how to clear water from the snorkel and how to put the facemask back on when treading water.
- Always be aware of your surroundings: don't let a current carry you too far from shore.
- NEVER let your keiki snorkel alone.
- Know the local weather conditions. Be aware of any postings on the beach and keep within the lifeguard's line of sight.
- Let your keiki snorkel at his/her own pace. For younger keiki, they can stay very close to shore and still see small fish and creatures at some beaches—especially Hanauma Bay.

starfish and green sea turtles. Try these spots for some of the best snorkeling on the island.

Just for laughs

Why are fish so smart?

Because they live in schools.

Hanauma Bay
Ever snorkeled inside of an ancient volcano? Hanauma Bay is the most famous snorkeling spot on O'ahu, with hundreds of different colorful fish. Snorkel rentals are available. Parking donation of $5 per car. Near Koko Head at 7455 Kalaniana'ole Highway.

Sign Hunt

While you're out on your adventures and excursions around Oʻahu, here's a car game you can play while driving to your next activity.

Try to find these signs. Add up your points at the end. Anyone can play and any number of kids can join. Whoever sees the sign first receives the points. They could be anywhere on the island, so keep your eyes peeled! Good luck.

A. (5 points)

C. (7 points)

BURGERLAND DRIVE IN
SUNRAY MARKET
Enjoy Coca-Cola

B. (3 points)

D. (5 points)

F. (5 points)

Island Paddler

honolulu

E. (3 points)

Kāhala Beach

The shallow reef all along Kāhala Beach can be good for snorkeling. No lifeguard or restrooms. Public accesses are all along Kāhala Avenue, try the one at Hunakai Street.

Ka'alāwai Beach (Also "Cromwells" or "Kaiko's" [Kaiko'o])

Get up close and personal with Hawai'i's underwater world. PHOTO © DOUGLAS PEEBLES

Shallow reef is good for snorkeling along the beach. A large protected tidepool at the east end is also good for snorkeling. No lifeguard or restrooms. Public access at the end of Kulamanu Street off Kāhala Avenue.

Lanikai Beach

Safe swimming with scattered coral heads on the north end of the beach. No lifeguard, nearest public restrooms at Kailua Boat Ramp. Park on Mokulua Drive, public beach accesses between private homes.

Waimea Bay

Swimming and snorkeling is only safe here during the summer months (May through August). Never swim here in the winter (October through April). Lifeguard on duty. 61-031 Kamehameha Highway.

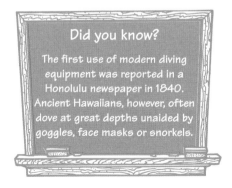

Did you know?

The first use of modern diving equipment was reported in a Honolulu newspaper in 1840. Ancient Hawaiians, however, often dove at great depths unaided by goggles, face masks or snorkels.

Pūpūkea Beach Park (Also "Shark's Cove")

During summer months only, snorkeling is good in the large, protected tidepool. Avoid the coral shelf at the edge where large waves often crash over the top. No lifeguard. Located on the North Shore at 59-727 Kamehameha Highway across from the Pūpūkea Foodland.

Buy some souvenirs of the sea at this Hale'iwa roadside stand.

Beachcombing

That stuff stuck between your toes is more than just plain old sand—take a closer look. You can collect beautiful shells, smooth sea glass, tiny crabs and lots of different kinds of seaweeds. Look for hidden treasures at the following O'ahu beaches.

PARENTS: Rough surf and shallow coral reefs are a good combination for bringing polished seashells to the beach. But beware, they usually don't make a good combination for safe swimming. Swimming at many of the following beaches is not recommended.

Banzai Beach (Also "Log Cabins")

Pukas and other shells can sometimes be found at Banzai or further down towards Pūpūkea at Log Cabins. During the winter, go at low tide. Lifeguard during the summer and on weekends, but swimming is not recommended. No restrooms. To get there, use the public right-of-way at the Pūpūkea end of Ke Waena Road.

Mokulēʻia Beach
Look for shells here at low tide. No lifeguard. Walk east along the beach from Mokulēʻia Beach Park at 68-919 Farrington Highway.

Kaunala Beach (Also "Velzyland")
Popular beachcombing spot. No lifeguard, and swimming is not recommended. Public access from the end of Oʻopuola Street at Sunset Point. Kaunala Beach will be on your right.

Turtle Bay
Coral and shells can be found on the beach fronting the Turtle Bay Resort, but swimming is not recommended because of shallow rocks and reefs offshore. No lifeguard. Turn in at the main hotel entrance and follow the signs that read "Shoreline Public Access." At the guard station ask for a parking pass for the public beach. This costs $1.50 for the day. 57-091 Kamehameha Highway between Kahuku and Sunset Beach.

Mālaekahana Beach (Also Mokuʻauia Beach on Goat Island)
Both Mālaekahana and Mokuʻauia beaches sometimes have coral and shells. On calm days at low tide you can wade across the reef to Goat Island. No lifeguard. Off Kamehameha Highway between Lāʻie and Kahuku.

Pounders Beach
Popular bodysurfing beach in Lāʻie where shells can be found. No

Building sandcastles or just playing in the sand is also a great way to spend the day here at Kailua Beach.

lifeguard, swimming is not recommended (try the north end if you must). Pounders is the section to the south, where bodyboarders hang out beside the rocky cliff. Swim on the north end if you must. Park in the Lāʻie Beach Park lot located off Kamehameha Highway just before the Polynesian Cultural Center when heading north.

Punaluʻu Beach Park
Search for treasures on this narrow beach during low tide. No lifeguard, but swimming is safe close in near the beach. 53-309 Kamehameha Highway.

Bellows Field Beach Park
Not a lot of shells, but seaweed and other ocean treasures can be found here. Wide, sandy beach with good bodysurfing conditions. Public access and lifeguards only on weekends. Take turn-off from Kalanianaʻole into Bellows Field and go through the gate.

Making Waves
When it gets too hot on the sand, cool your tootsies off in the water. When you're chillin' out in Hawaiʻi you have an endless list of watersports and activities to choose from.

Outrigger canoe paddling
There's no better way to spend the summer than paddling on a canoe club team. There are at least 17 clubs that practice around Oʻahu. If you can't make the commitment, you can always spend a day canoe surfing in Waikīkī.

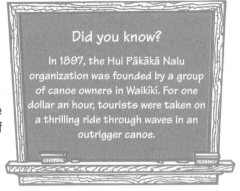

Have you bodysurfed at Kalama Beach Park yet? Don't miss out on the fun. Photo courtesy of Kailua Sailboards and Kayaks, inc.

SURF'S UP!

ACROSS

2. On a surfboard, to get out to where the waves are breaking, you have to _____.

5. Sometimes you have to dive _____ incoming waves when paddling out.

6. Some people wear these on their feet when bodyboarding.

8. The one animal you don't want to see when you're out surfing.

11. Surfers want to catch some _____.

12. When waiting for a wave, you can ____ on your board.

13. You have to ____ the board down the wave by shifting your weight.

15. Snorkelers swim around this to see fish, but if your board scrapes across it, it's not a good thing.

17. You don't necessarily need a _____ to surf.

DOWN

1. People who surf are called _____.

3. It's safer not to surf after _____.

4. ♪♪ _____ go surf! ♪♪♪

7. Pipeline is where on the Island of O'ahu?

9. You wear this surfing if it's cold or if you don't want to get sunburned.

10. A wave before it breaks.

14. Some people catch waves in this one-man or two-man craft.

16. Surfing is _____!

Spend time with your friendly neighborhood firemen and learn how to surf, too! Photo courtesy of Hawaiian Fire Surf School.

To join a canoe paddling team, contact the Oʻahu Hawaiian Canoe Racing Association (OHCRA): 261-6615, or visit www.ohcra.com or www.hawaiianh2o.com to find the club nearest to you.

Outrigger canoe rides and lessons:
Sheraton Moana Surfrider: 922-3111
Outrigger Reef on the Beach: 923-3111
Outrigger Waikīkī on the Beach: 923-0711

Bodysurfing and bodyboarding

The best spots for kids to go bodysurfing and bodyboarding

Bodyboarding at Kailua Beach.

have small-to-medium shorebreak waves and sandy bottoms. Try the beaches in Waimānalo: Sherwoods, Bellows, and Waimānalo Beach Park. Another favorite for kids is Kalama Beach Park in Kailua (see info and directions in the Beaches section, page 6).

Surfing

Oʻahu is well-known for having killer surf spots. Some of the mellower breaks for kids are listed below.

Kailua Shorebreak
The sandy stretch along Kalāheo Avenue to the north of Kailua Beach Park. No lifeguard.

Flat Island
Good longboarding spot to the right of Flat Island. No lifeguard. Near the entrance to Lanikai by the Kailua boat ramp at the beginning of Mokulua Drive.

If you don't know how to surf, take lessons in Haleʻiwa.

Kaupō Beach Park (Also "Kumu Cove" or "Cockroach Bay")
Small rolling waves in the cove to the right of the old pier make this a good spot for novice surfers and longboarders. No lifeguard. Across from Oceanic Institute in Waimānalo at 41-401 Kalanianaʻole Highway.

Waikīkī Beach
Thousands of locals and visitors have learned to surf on Waikīkī's mellow waves. Lifeguards year round. Surfboard rentals and lessons are available near the Waikīkī Beach Center. All along Kalākaua Avenue, Waikīkī Beach Center at 2435 Kalākaua Avenue.

Take Lessons!

Many of these companies offer surfing lessons (under $100) for kids ages 7 and up, as long as they can swim:

Aloha School of Surf: 778-6227
(www.alohasurf.org)
Aloha Spirit of Hawai'i: 921-0110
Eco-Surf Tours on the North Shore: 638-9503
Hans Hedeman Surf School: 923-7779/924-7778
(www.hhsurf.com)
Hawai'i Surf Academy (private or group): 382-6778
(www.aulani.com/surf.htm)
Hawaiian Fire Surf School (run by firefighters): 384-8855/1-888-955-7873 (www.hawaiianfire.com)
Hawaiian Watersports: 262-5483/255-4352
(www.hawaiianwatersports.com)

Take surf lessons in Waikīkī—it's not just for tourists, you know. PHOTO © DOUGLAS PEEBLES.

Never tried surfing before? Now is a great time to start. Attend a surf camp or take lessons. There's nothing like feeling the rush of riding a wave—great fun for girls and boys. PHOTO © DOUGLAS PEEBLES.

Kailua Sailboards and Kayaks: 262-2555
North Shore Eco-Surf Tours: 638-9503
Outrigger Waikīkī on the Beach Hotel: 923-0711
Sheraton Moana Surfrider Hotel: 922-3111
Sunset Suzy's Surf Lessons: 781-2692
    (www.sunsetsuzy.com)
Surf and Sea on the North Shore: 637-9887
TEC Surf.net: 232-0900
Waikīkī Beach Activities, Inc. at Hilton Hawaiian Village: 951-4088

The statue of Duke Kahanamoku,
found in Waikīkī, is often draped with lei.

Haleʻiwa surfboard rental stand.

Surf Camps

Rochelle Ballard's Surf Camp for Girls

Girls ages 8–19 can hang out with female pro-surfers like Rochelle Ballard, Megan Abubo, and Keala Kennelly in Mokulēʻia for three days of non-stop surfing. Camp is one weekend a year in January or February. $40 covers all expenses. www.rochelleballard.com • Ph: 283-7144

Did you know?

Olympic champion and Ambassador of Aloha Duke Kahanamoku surfed with a solid koa wood surfboard, which weighed over 150 pounds.

North Shore Surf Camp by Kamaʻaina Kids

Stay overnight in cabins at Camp Timberline in the Waianae Mountains and spend your days surfing the North Shore with Surf-N-Sea instructors. Other activities include kayaking, windsurfing, archery, ropes courses, and campfire storytelling. Sessions are six days long

Water Sports

```
C K I T E S U R F S
A B S N O R K E L A
N O W A T E R S K I
O D G I N A C U G L
E Y U R N R K R D S
V B W A T D L F E O
L O P A R A S A I L
K A Y A K F W U K S
W R D I V I N G R R
H D F G N I H S I F
```

Try to find all these great ocean sports. Some are horizontal, vertical,
diagonal and backwards. Circle the ones you find.

windsurf	canoe
water ski	fishing
parasail	bodyboard
surf	kitesurf
kayak	sail
diving	snorkel

and run June through July. For kids ages 10–17. $625 per session, or
$600 for kamaʻaina. www.kamaainakids.com/summer03/xteenf.html • Ph:
262-4538

Hawaiʻi Surf Academy
Kids of all ages can sign up for six days and five nights of surfing, camping
and fun on the North Shore under the direction of pro-surfers and certified
lifeguards. Camp in tents or homestay with instructors' families. Sessions
are year-round. $1,450 per person for full six days. www.aulani.com/
surf.htm • Ph: 382-6778

Skimboarding

Riding the waves is great, but have you ever ridden the sand? You can skimboard anywhere where the beach is flat, sandy (meaning not rocky), and where the waves break enough to cover the sand with a slick wet layer of water, but aren't too rough. Try Kailua Beach, Waimānalo Beach Park, Sherwoods, Bellows, and Waimea (ONLY in the summertime from May through July).

Parasailing

After spending so much time IN the water, why don't you try sailing ABOVE it? Parasailing is really exciting—you and a friend are buckled into a large sled that climbs to a

Kayaking with mom or dad is a great way to spend the day. Photo courtesy of Kailua Sailboards and Kayaks, inc.

hundred feet above the water under an enormous parachute. A motorboat pulls you with a rope down below. There's nothing like it. Parasailing adventures are offered in Waikīkī and in Hawai'i Kai.

Aloha Parasail: 521-2446
Hawaiian Parasail: 591-1280
Sea Breeze Parasailing: 396-0100
Super Hawai'i Adventures, Inc.: 394-2238
Waikīkī Watersports: 735-6474

Kayaking

Kids can kayak too! Lessons and kayak rentals are available at:
Hawaiian Watersports: 262-5483/255-4352
   (www.hawaiianwatersports.com)
Kailua Sailboards and Kayaks: 262-2555
Kayak Oahu Adventures: 923-0539
Two Good Kayaks Hawai'i Inc.: 262-5656
Waikīkī Beach Activities at Hilton Hawaiian Village: 951-4088

Water skiing/wakeboarding

Create your own waves on a wakeboard or waterskis! Kids ages 6 and up can take lessons or rent equipment at Hawai'i Sports Wakeboard and Waterski, 395-3773 (www.hisports.com).

Kitesurfing

The latest craze in water sports, kitesurfing is like a mix between flying a kite and windsurfing. Kids who are good swimmers (ages 8 and up) can take lessons:

Hawaiian Watersports: 262-5483/255-4352
   (www.hawaiianwatersports.com)

Kite surfing at Kailua Beach.

Kailua Sailboards and Kayaks: 262-2555
Kitehigh: 637-0025

Windsurfing

Can kids windsurf? Well, when he was only 13 years old, Robby Naish of Kailua became windsurfing world champion! Give it a try. To rent equipment or take lessons, contact one of these companies:

> ### Did you know?
>
> Windsurfing, also called boardsailing, freesailing and sailboarding apparently originated in Hawai'i. Tom Blake, an innovator in surfboard design, experimented with various sailing rigs attached to his surfboard down at Waikīkī Beach in the 1930s.

Hawaiian Watersports: 262-5483/ 255-4352
(www.hawaiianwatersports.com)
Kailua Sailboards and Kayaks: 262-2555
Naish Hawaii: 262-6068
Surf and Sea: 637-9887
North Shore Eco-Surf Tours: 638-9503

Hans Hedeman Surf School: 923-7779/924-7778
(www.hhsurf.com)

Sailing

Kids ages 8 and up can learn to be junior sailors at a local yacht club. You don't have to be a member of a club to take lessons. Visit the Hawai'i Youth Sailing Association website at www.holoholo.org/hysa/index.html, or contact the following clubs:

Kāne'ohe Yacht Club: 247-4121
Waikīkī Yacht Club: 949-7141/955-4405
Hawai'i Yacht Club: 949-7547 (xt. 16)
Pearl Harbor/Rainbow Bay Marina: 471-9680
Pacific Yacht Club: 624-5484
Hickam Harbor: 449-5215
University of Hawai'i: 956-5177
Free Spirit Sailing Club (only with an adult): 943-0017

Ahoy matey at the Ala Wai Yacht Harbor.

Visit a Neighborhood Pool

Tired of the beach? Did you know there are at least 16 public pools on Oʻahu that you can swim in for **FREE**? On a hot summer day, jumping into your local pool can be just as refreshing as a dip in the ocean. Bring some goggles and a beachball for relay races and games. And the best part: no sand stuck in your swimsuit.

Booth Pool: 522-7037
Kailua Pool: 266-7661
Kalihi Valley Pool: 832-7814
Kāneʻohe Pool: 233-7311
Kanewai Pool: 733-7365
Kapaolono Pool: 733-7369

Just for laughs

A lemon and an orange were on the diving board. The orange jumped off but the lemon didn't. Why?

Because it was yellow.

Cool off your tootsies in a local swimming pool.

Manana Pool: 453-7556
Mānoa Pool: 988-6868 McCully Pool: 973-7268
Moanalua Pool: 831-7106
Pālolo Valley Pool: 733-7362
Pearl City Pool: 453-7552
Wahiawā Pool: 621-0857
Waialua Pool: 637-6061
Waikele Pool: 678-0872
Waipahu Pool: 671-7911

Sign up for Swim School!

Lēʻahi Swim School
Kids from 6 months old and up can learn water survival skills and swimming in a fun and safe environment. All teachers are lifeguard certified by the Red Cross. Pool is located at 2707 Pāmoa Road at St. Francis School. www.leahiswimschool.com • Ph: 735-1666

Fun Idea!

Pretend you're in the Olympics and challenge your friends to swimming races in the pool. Have your mom or dad time you. Just be sure to respect all the rules of the pool area.

Did you know?

The first full-scale swimming pools on Oʻahu were built for Punahou School and Kamehameha School for Boys in the late 1880s.

PICNIC IN THE PARK

On a warm, sunny day, pack up your soccer ball, frisbee, a book and some snacks and head for a green grassy park. O'ahu has hundreds of small neighborhood parks for a quiet afternoon, and lots of large, happening parks where people gather to barbecue, play sports and hang out with friends and family. Visit one of the many lush botanical gardens where you can find gigantic banyan trees, rare fruits and flowers and some really strange and unusual plants. Some parks—like Haiku Gardens in Kāne'ohe—have streams where you can find creatures of all sorts, from pinchy crayfish to squiggly tadpoles and hopping toads. (All parks listed are **FREE**; botanical gardens may charge admission.)

Tiny Tots Park Program

Preschoolers can meet up with other kids their age at Tiny Tots, a **FREE** program offered by the City and County at district parks all around O'ahu. Kids can play games, sing songs and learn new crafts. Mom or Dad can meet other parents with preschool-age kids in the area. Check it out!

Hawai'i Kai to McCully: 973-7250
Makiki to 'Aiea: 522-7070
Pearl City to Wai'anae: 671-0561
Waialua to Waimānalo: 233-7300

Fun Idea!

Plan a trip to the park and celebrate the letter P: have a picinic of poi, pineapple, peanut butter, purple punch and play!

Kapi'olani Park

Picnic in the Park

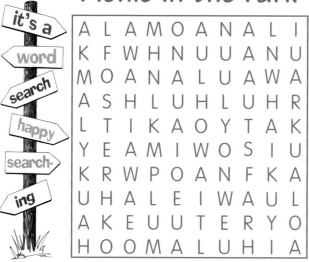

```
A L A M O A N A L I
K F W H N U U A N U
M O A N A L U A W A
A S H L U H L U H R
L T I K A O Y T A K
Y E A M I W O S I U
K R W P O A N F K A
U H A L E I W A U L
A K E U U T E R Y O
H O O M A L U H I A
```

it's a word search happy search- ing

Try to find all these parks and gardens on O'ahu. Some are horizontal, vertical, diagonal and backwards. Circle the ones you find.

Kapi'olani   Lyon
Ho'omaluhia   Kualoa
Hale'iwa   Ala Moana
Wahiawā   Nu'uanu
Foster   Ha'ikū
Moanalua

Did you know?

Kapi'olani Park, named after Queen Kap'iolani, was opened with a grand celebration by King Kalākaua on Kamehameha Day in 1877.

SOUTH SHORE/TOWN
Kapi'olani Park
This huge 140-acre park next to Diamond Head is a local favorite for barbecues, soccer, frisbee, tennis, archery, flying kites and just about everything else. Lots of open space and big banyan trees. Next to the Honolulu Zoo between Monsarrat and Kalākaua Avenues.

Sit and picnic with your family in Kapi'olani Park under a shady tree after a morning at the beach.

Moanalua Gardens
Huge monkeypod trees shade this grassy park. During the summer, the Prince Lot Hula Festival is held here. 1401 Mahiole Street.

Ala Moana Beach Park
Another favorite local hangout with snack bars, picnic areas, bridges and paths—right on the beach. Across the street from Ala Moana Shopping Center at 1201 Ala Moana Boulevard.

Magic Island
Magic Island is often crowded with kids and families during the weekend. With walkways, benches and open spaces, its a fun place to barbecue. At the east end of Ala Moana Beach Park, 1201 Ala Moana Boulevard.

Sand Island State Recreation Area
Coastal park with a small sand beach. End of Sand Island Access Road off Nimitz Highway.

Kaka'ako Waterfront Park
Large coastal park with paved pathways that make this a great place to rollerskate or skateboard. End of 'Āhui and 'Ohe Streets off Ala Moana Boulevard.

Waialae Beach Park
Small beach park. End of Kahala Avenue. 4925 Kāhala Avenue.

Just for laughs

How can you tell the difference between trees?

Listen to their barks.

Moanalua Gardens

Lēʻahi and Mākālei Parks

Two small parks on Diamond Head Road that have great views of the ocean. Mākālei Park has beach access. Located on the stretch of Diamond Head Road between the lighthouse and Kapiʻolani Park.

EASTSIDE

Kahana Valley State Park

Wild, forested valley with trails for hiking. Nice picnic spot in coconut grove, beach park across the highway. 52-222 Kamehameha Highway.

Headed for a park and curious about learning new things? Contact the Hawaiʻi Nature Center for information about their family programs and make a day of it. Photo courtesy of the Hawaiʻi Nature Center.

Kakaʻako Waterfront Park has a great pathway for biking and an open lawn for picnicing while watching the surf.

Kualoa County Regional Park

Big, grassy park on the coast across from Mokoli'i Island (Chinaman's Hat). Nice place to picnic and camp. 49-600 area of Kamehameha Highway.

He'eia State Park

Coastal park next to historic fishpond. 46-465 Kamehameha Highway.

Ha'ikū Gardens

Beautiful lush gardens with lily ponds, flowers and trees. Catch some crayfish in the stream and watch the peacocks dance. 46-336 Ha'ikū Road in Kāne'ohe.

NORTH SHORE

Hale'iwa Beach Park

Big, grassy park with a baseball diamond and basketball and volleyball courts. Right on the beach in Hale'iwa. 62-449 Kamehameha Highway.

Sandy Beach Park is a great location for flying kites—especially when the wind is kicking.

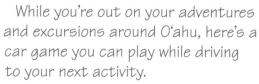

Sign Hunt

While you're out on your adventures and excursions around O'ahu, here's a car game you can play while driving to your next activity.

Try to find these signs. Add up your points at the end. Anyone can play and any number of kids can join. Whoever sees the sign first receives the points. They could be anywhere on the island, so keep your eyes peeled! Good luck.

A. (5 points)

B. (3 points)

C. (5 points)

D. (3 points)

E. (3 points)

F. (3 points)

Wahiawā Botanical Garden.

Botanical Gardens

Wahiawā Botanical Garden
Walk through a rainforest in this wild valley garden. 1396 California Avenue; 621-7321. **FREE**

Koko Crater Botanic Garden
Hot and dry garden inside of Koko Crater with cacti and exotic African plants. Self-

Try look!
(it's a car game for kids)

While you're in the car, going to the park, see who can find these things. Whoever finds it first gets the points.

A plumeria tree	2 points
A fire hydrant	2 points
A dog in a car or truck	5 points
A Hawaiian flag	8 points

Safety First!

Oʻahu's parks are fun for everyone. Keiki can fly kites, play sports, picnic, or sit under a tree with a good book. There are numerous small neighborhood parks, large open-area parks, and gardens where you can find the most beautiful plants around. See Native Hawaiian plants in all their glory. Witness hybrids beyond belief. But keep these safety tips in mind:

Park safety and consideration
- Always keep an eye on your keiki. For the very young ones, make sure they understand to stay away from main roads and to not wander off.
- NEVER let your keiki go to park restrooms alone. Always have an adult accompany them.
- Practice sun safety (see page 8).
- If you are visiting the various gardens around the island, take care not to destroy any of the vegetation—keep to the paths provided.
- Take precautions when it comes to insects: be aware of your surroundings. Bring insect repellent.
- Don't leave valuables in your car. Unfortunately, visitors and rented cars are targets for thieves.
- Respect the ʻāina (land). If you're picnicing, bring a bag to collect your trash when you leave.

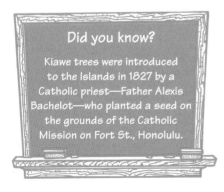

Did you know?
Kiawe trees were introduced to the Islands in 1827 by a Catholic priest—Father Alexis Bachelot—who planted a seed on the grounds of the Catholic Mission on Fort St., Honolulu.

guided tour only. Next to Koko Crater Stables, access from Kealahou Street in Hawaiʻi Kai. **FREE**

Lyon Arboretum
Botanical garden in the back of Mānoa Valley, lots of tropical and native Hawaiian plants. Call ahead for a tour, or sign up for a kids' summer science and

Foster Botanical Gardens.

nature class. Bring mosquito repellent, rain gear and shoes. Donations requested. 3860 Mānoa Road • Ph: 988-0456.

Foster Botanical Garden

Honolulu's oldest botanical garden with trees more than 150 years old! Bring mosquito repellent and shoes. Entrance fee for kids 6–12, $1; 13 and older, $5 ($3 for kama'aina with ID); **FREE** for kids 5 and under. 50 North Vineyard Boulevard • Ph: 522-7060.

Ho'omaluhia Botanical Garden

Large, 400-acre botanical garden and park in the back of Kāne'ohe. Camping with permit allowed. Guided hikes and night walks offered on weekends, call ahead to register. Bring rain gear, mosquito repellent and shoes. 45-680 Luluku Road • Ph: 233-7323. **FREE**

Lili'uokalani Botanical Garden

These were once the favorite picnic grounds for Queen Lili'uokalani. Lots of native Hawaiian plants.
Between North Kuakini and School Streets in downtown Honolulu.

Lili'uokalani Botanical Garden.

Fun Idea!
Take a plant ID book with you on your trip to the botanical garden and see how many flowers or plants you can identify.

MUSEUMS, TOURS & ADVENTURES

What do you do when it's cloudy outside, or you're just plain tired of being out in the sun? Put on your shoes and your thinking cap. There's a lot to do indoors at O'ahu's many museums—from making gigantic bubbles at the Children's Discovery Center and exploring outer space at the Bishop Museum Planetarium to playing with a pot-belly pig at the Honolulu Petting Zoo.

PD = parent dropoff allowed
PR = parental supervision required

Let's Get Artsy

Artsy fartsy, you say? Art museums aren't as stuffy as you might think. There are lots of things for kids to do at O'ahu's art museums. Roll up your sleeves and get crafty.

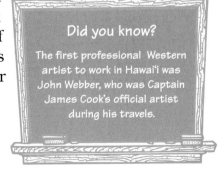

Did you know?

The first professional Western artist to work in Hawai'i was John Webber, who was Captain James Cook's official artist during his travels.

Children create with clay at the Contemporary Museum's
Art Spree. PHOTO COURTESY OF THE CONTEMPORARY MUSEUM.

Contemporary Art Museum (PD for some classes)

Modern art museum with beautiful gardens, cafe, cool outdoor sculptures, and a spooky display by David Hockney that takes kids deep into an enchanted forest. Special programs for kids of all ages include art and poetry workshops and Expression Sessions (for ages 5–12) led by artists from the community. Topics range from tie-dyeing banners to surfboard-making demonstrations. Museum admission is **FREE** for kids 12 and under; adult admission is $5, but **FREE** to all ages on the third Thursday of each month. Closed Mondays. 2411 Makiki Heights Drive • www.tcmhi.org • Ph: 526-0232

Hawai'i State Art Museum

Located on the second floor of the No. 1 Capitol District Building, the Hawai'i State Art Museum houses the unique art of Hawai'i's own artists. Head downtown and visit this Spanish Mission-style building and see how the Islands' unique mix of cultures is blended into various art pieces.

Academy Art Center at Linekona

See Hawaiian kapa, quilts, Japanese shizu embroidery and raku pottery. Admission is **FREE**. Open Tuesday through Saturday from 10 a.m. to 4 p.m. 250 South Hotel Street • www.state.hi.us/sfca • Ph: 586-0900

Honolulu Academy of Arts   (PD for some classes)

The museum itself is a beautiful old building with permanent collections from Hawai'i, Asia, Oceania, Africa, the Americas and Europe. Across the street, the Academy Art Center at Linekona offers spring, summer and fall studio art classes in drawing, painting, printmaking, jewelry, ceramics, weaving and other arts for kids (grades K–12) and adults. Young People's Art Exhibitions are on display at the end of each class session. Call 532-8741 for more info about kids' classes. Museum admission is **FREE** for kids 12 and under; $7 for adults; $4 for students 13 and up. Closed Mondays. 900 South Beretania Street in Honolulu • www.honolulu academy.org • Ph: 532-8701

UH Mānoa Art Gallery

Check out the gallery on the UH Mānoa campus to see some cool, multicultural exhibits. Closed Saturdays. **FREE** www.hawaii.edu/artgallery • Ph: 956-6888

Windward Community College

"Play in Clay" pottery classes for kids only, parents and kids (age 5 and up), and teens. Also, check out WCC's Imaginarium, a planetarium that has 3-D interactive star-gazing shows. Classes are $10–20, call 235-7433 to register. Imaginarium is $3 for kids 12 and under; $5 for adults. 45-720 Kea'ahala Road in Kāne'ohe • www. wcc.hawaii.edu • Ph: 235-7400

An exhibit from the University of Hawai'i Art Gallery—The Art of Asian Costume. Photo courtesy of the University of Hawai'i Art Gallery.

Animals, Animals Everywhere

Have you ever seen a hippopotamus up close? Heard a Hawaiian monk seal bark? Get in touch with your "wild side" at one of O'ahu's creature features.

Honolulu Zoo (PD for some programs)

See the big cats and the Burmese python, hear the howler monkeys howl. Get up close and personal with llamas, lizards and an enormous cow at the petting zoo. Kids ages 5–11 can sign up for Zoo Day Camp to go behind the scenes and see how the animals are fed and cared for. There are Moonlight Tours for kids (5 and up) and adults—you can even camp out on the zoo lawn! Keiki (ages 6–10) and Junior (11 and up) Zookeeper programs let kids practice caring for the animals. Art in the Zoo classes (ages 5–11) and special ZOOper Birthday Parties make the zoo a fun-filled place for kids year-round. You can even check out some great art along the zoo fence on weekends. **FREE** admission for kids 5 and under; ages 6–12, $1; adults, $6; kama'aina with ID, $4. Special keiki programs cost extra. 151 Kapahulu Avenue • www.honoluluzoo.org • Ph: 971-7171

Waikīkī Aquarium (PR)

There are more than 2,500 different plants and animals at the Waikīkī Aquarium. Watch rare Hawaiian monk seals playing in their outdoor pool, or see jellyfish and sharks up close behind the

The zoo is fun for all ages.

Programs for the youngest learners are among the Waikīkī Aquarium's most popular offerings. Small Fry classes are designed for adults with 1- to 3-year olds. PHOTO COURTESY OF THE WAIKĪKĪ AQUARIUM.

glass. Touch and hold sea urchins and starfish in the outdoor reef exhibit. Kids (ages 5 and up) and parents can also sign up for day and night reef walks, marine science sleepovers, after dark aquarium tours and off-island expeditions. Aquarium admission is **FREE** for kids 12 and under; $3.50 for ages 13–17; $7 for visitors; $5 for kama'aina, military, students and seniors. 2777 Kalākaua Avenue • www.waikikiaquarium.com • Ph: 923-9741

Sea Life Park

Walk through the Hawaiian reef aquarium at Sea Life Park and you'll be face to face with sharks, stingrays, sea turtles and schools of fish! Check out the dolphin shows and the turtle and sea bird sanc-

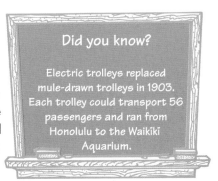

Did you know?

Electric trolleys replaced mule-drawn trolleys in 1903. Each trolley could transport 56 passengers and ran from Honolulu to the Waikīkī Aquarium.

Get up close and personal with marine life at Sea Life Park's Splash University. Photo courtesy of Atlantis Adventures.

tuaries, throw fish to the outdoor sea lions and touch and hold creatures from the reef. Kids 4 and up can get wet in the Stingray Lagoon and learn how dolphins are trained. Older kids can swim with the dolphins (13 and up) and walk underwater in the reef aquarium (12 and older). Or have a SEA-SATIONAL birthday party at Sea Life Park. Admission for kids 4–12 is $13; 13 and up and adults, $25. 41-202 Kalaniana'ole Highway in Waimānalo • www.sealifepark hawaii.com • Ph: 259-7933

Stingrays and sharks swim by curious keiki at the Sea Life Park aquarium.

Dinosaur Exhibit at Honolulu Community College

Did you know that a tyrannosaurus rex was 20 feet tall? See a full-sized T-rex skull and leg up close on the tour of Hawai'i's only dinosaur exhibit. Replicas of real dinosaur skulls and bones are from the American Museum of Natural History in New York. **FREE** 874 Dillingham Boulevard • www.hcc.hawaii.edu/dinos/dinos.1.html • Ph: 845-9211

Get Back to Nature

"Mālama i ka 'āina" means "caring for the land"—something that the Native Hawaiians felt was very important. Take off your slippers and feel the sand between your toes. Lie down in your backyard at night and study the stars. When you stop and think about it, there are so many questions to be answered about the world around you: What makes the sky blue? How are rainbows made? Where does our drinking water come from? Check out some of the great places on O'ahu where you can learn more about the magic and mystery of nature.

Hawai'i Nature Center

Learn about Hawai'i's unique plants and animals and slide down through a volcano! The Hawai'i Nature Center offers kid-focused guided hikes and nature projects for the whole family. **FREE** 2131 Makiki Heights Drive • www.hawaiinaturecenter. org • Ph: 955-0100

What are they looking at? Find out at the Hawai'i Nature Center! Photo courtesy of the Hawai'i Nature Center.

Explore nature with the Hawai'i Nature Center—they have family programs perfect for curious keiki. Photo courtesy of the Hawai'i Nature Center.

Bishop Museum Planetarium and Natural History Hall

Sit back and be amazed by the panoramic shows at the Planetarium. You can learn about the stars, astronauts in space, Polynesian explorers or scientists on the top of snowy Mauna Kea. Also, learn how plants, animals and insects evolved in Hawai'i's unique environment in the Natural History Hall. A walk through the Hawaiian Science Garden teaches about traditional Hawaiian taro farming and fishponds. **FREE** for kids 3 and under; kids ages 4–12 and seniors, $12; adults, $15. Special rates for kama'aina with ID. 1525 Bernice Street • www.bishopmuseum.org • Ph: 847-3511

Did you know?

Bishop Museum was founded in 1889 and was opened to the public in 1892.

Dress up like a squid or a starfish at the Hawai'i Children's Discovery Center.

Hawai'i Children's Discovery Center

Where do all the people of Hawai'i come from? Get to know the different cultures that make Hawai'i a unique place with some hands-on activities. You can also blow gigantic bubbles, dress up in costumes from different countries, walk on the ocean floor, play volleyball with a robot and climb inside the human body at the amazing Children's Discovery Center. Fun for the whole family. Admission is $6.75 for kids 2–17; $8 for adults. Closed Mondays. 111 Ohe Street across from Kaka'ako Waterfront Park • www.discoverycenter hawaii.org • Ph: 524-KIDS

Navigating Change at the Maritime Center

Walk on a pretend atoll and get to know the wildlife that lives there. Find out what you can do to help save Hawai'i's land and sea environments. Exhibit is at the Hawai'i Maritime Center at Pier 7 on Honolulu Harbor.

The Maritime Center next to Aloha Tower.

Kids 6 and under **FREE**; ages 6–17, $4.50; adults, $7.50. www.navigatingchange.org • Ph: 536-6373

Waimea Arboretum and Botanical Garden

Explore the 36 gardens in the back of Waimea Valley, or take a kid's Jungle Trek into the rainforest. You can get up close to butterflies and learn about the rare and unique plants of the world. Kids 4–12, $12; 13 and up, $24. Half price for kamaʻaina with ID. Located in Waimea Valley Adventure Park at 59-864 Kamehameha Highway • Ph: 638-8655

Lyon Arboretum Summer Science Classes (PD)

Kids ages 6–12 can sign up for summer science and nature classes at Lyon Arboretum. Go on hikes and picnics, learn to make paper and cook

Foster Botanical Garden.

Rumble in the Jungle

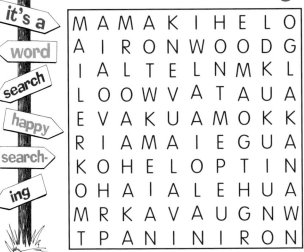

it's a word search happy search-ing

M	A	M	A	K	I	H	E	L	O
A	I	R	O	N	W	O	O	D	G
I	A	L	T	E	L	N	M	K	L
L	O	O	W	V	A	T	A	U	A
E	V	A	K	U	A	M	O	K	K
R	I	A	M	A	I	E	G	U	A
K	O	H	E	L	O	P	T	I	N
O	H	A	I	A	L	E	H	U	A
M	R	K	A	V	A	U	G	N	W
T	P	A	N	I	N	I	R	O	N

Try to find all these trees and plants on O'ahu. Some are horizontal, vertical, diagonal, and backwards. Circle the ones you find.

'ilima
koa
lakana
guava
ironwood
kiawe

maile
'ohelo
ti
ohaialehua
panini

food straight from the garden. Bring a lunch and rain gear, mosquito repellent and shoes. 3860 Mānoa Road • www.hawaii.edu/lyonarboretum/ • Ph: 988-0456

Ho'omaluhia Botanical Garden
Walk through this rainforest garden to learn about tropical plants from around the world. Bring rain gear, mosquito repellent and walking shoes. Guided hikes and "catch and release" family fishing on weekends, call ahead to register. 45-680 Luluku Road • Ph: 233-7323. **FREE**

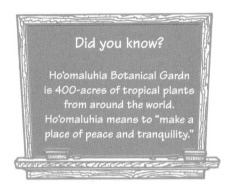

Foster Botanical Garden

Get to know giant palms, colorful orchids and some incredibly old and rare trees. Entrance fee for kids 6–12, $1; 13 and older, $5 ($3 for kama'aina with ID); **FREE** for kids 5 and under. 50 North Vineyard Boulevard • Ph: 522-7060

Koko Crater Botanic Garden

Hot and dry garden inside of Koko Crater with cacti and African plants. Self-guided tour only. Next to Koko Crater Stables, access from Kealahou Street in Hawai'i Kai. **FREE**

Wahiawā Botanical Garden

Walk through a rainforest in this wild valley garden and learn about plants from Hawai'i and around the world—they even have a chewing gum tree! Call ahead for a guided tour. 1396 California Avenue • Ph: 621-7321 **FREE**

Lili'uokalani Botanical Garden

These were once the favorite picnic grounds for Queen Lili'uokalani. Lots of native Hawaiian plants. Between North Kuakini and School Streets in downtown Honolulu.

Try look!
(it's a car game for kids)

While you're in the car, on your way to explore O'ahu, see who can find these things. Whoever finds it first gets the points.

A blue truck	2 points
The word ALOHA	2 points
Someone wearing a lei	5 points
Got _____? sticker	8 points

Honolulu Botanical Gardens Activities and Events

Kids can take Mom and Dad to fun events at botanical gardens all around O'ahu. Learn how to make haku leis, plant gardens and

HAWAIIAN LANGUAGE 101

ACROSS

1. child
4. taboo
5. hello/goodbye/love
7. finished
8. finished work
9. goodness
10. hurry-go
12. turtle

DOWN

1. taro
2. think / smart
3. thank you
5. goodbye
6. one more time
7. cat
9. drum
11. four

Just for laughs

Why did the gecko
cross the road?

The chicken didn't
feel like it.

go on family hikes. Find out what special events are planned on the community calendar at: www. co.honolulu.hi.us/parks/hbg/calendar.htm • Ph: 537-1708/522-7064

Learn About Hawai'i's History

What do you think Hawai'i was like 100 years ago? There were not many cars back then, and definitely no TVs or computers! Hawai'i's last queen, Lili'uokalani, still lived in Honolulu. But what about 1,000 years ago? Back then, Native Hawaiian chiefs ruled the islands. People worshiped gods and goddesses at stone temples and offered them gifts and sacrifices. Well, times have changed, but pieces of Hawai'i's exciting past are still around—maybe even in your own neigh-

Learn more about the 'āina and see how taro is planted. Photo courtesy of the Hawai'i Nature Center.

WHAT DO YOU KNOW ABOUT HAWAI'I?

ACROSS

1. This volcano on the Island of Hawai'i means "white mountain."
6. Cloth made from bark (tapa).
8. The youngest island in the Hawaiian chain.
9. A gourd instrument used in hula.
10. Number of stripes in the Hawaiian flag.
11. Hawaiian cowboy.
12. "Ua mau ke ea o ka 'aina ika pono" is Hawai'i's state _____.
13. Hawai'i's state bird.
14. Hawaiian word for delicious.

DOWN

2. _____ nuts can be strung into lei.
3. Mount Wai'ale'ale is on this island.
4. The Gathering Place
5. State anthem
7. Rock art
12. The Valley Isle

borhood! Take a trip back in time and discover what Hawaiʻi's history is all about.

Sacred Hawaiian Places

These are places that will give you a peek at what Hawaiʻi was like way back when Polynesians still ruled the Islands.

PARENTS: The sacred sites listed in this section are important parts of Hawaiʻi's heritage. Please make sure children show respect to all sites and structures. Do not take or move any lava rocks from historic sites. Many people still honor these Hawaiian sites with offerings—a lei or lava rocks wrapped in tī leaves. Please obey all signs and do not touch the offerings. Mahalo!

Kualoa Ranch and Regional Park
Kualoa was a very sacred place to the Native Hawaiians. Today, the Kualoa Ranch is a fun place where families can tour the movie set of *Jurassic Park,* go horseback riding (kids 10 and up), and take kayak tours (ages 12 and up) out to Mokoliʻi Island, also called Chinaman's Hat. Call 237-7321 to schedule activities. 49-560 Kamehameha Highway in Kaʻaʻawa • www.kualoa.com
• Ph: 237-8515

Puʻu o Mahuka Heiau
Visit a real Hawaiian temple, or heiau, where Hawaiian priests made human sacrifices to the war god, Kū. You can walk all the way around the huge lava rock heiau,

Do you know the story behind the Wizard Stones in Waikīkī?

but walking on the rocks is kapu, or forbidden. The lava rocks that you see wrapped in tī leaves are offerings made by people who still honor the Hawaiian gods. Please do not touch offerings. Take Pūpūkea Road (next to the Foodland) up the hill from Kamehameha Highway, follow the sign

The Birthstones in Wahiawā.

to the Puʻu o Mahuka Heiau State Monument and drive down the access road. **FREE**

Nuʻuanu Pali Lookout
Look over the edge of a 1,000-foot cliff where thousands of Native Hawaiian warriors fell to their deaths during a famous battle with Kamehameha the Great. The strong winds here feel as if they could pick you up off your feet—hang on tight! Take a short paved hike down the Old Pali Highway, off to the right of the lookout. Located off the Pali Highway near the tunnels, access roads are well marked with signs in both directions. **FREE**

Hōkūleʻa Polynesian Voyaging Canoe
Step on board the Hokuleʻa and see how Native Hawaiian navigators sailed the Pacific using only the stars, wind and ocean currents. The Hōkūleʻa has traveled all around Polynesia using these traditional Hawaiian techniques, and its success proved to the world that the ancient Hawaiians were very skilled sailors on the open sea. Tours are offered through the Hawaiʻi Maritime Center at Pier 7 on Honolulu Harbor. Kids 6 and under **FREE**; ages 6–17, $4.50; adults, $7.50. www.bishopmuseum. org/hokulea. html • Ph: 536-6373

Kūkaniloko Birthstones State Monument
In the old days, Hawaiian royalty gave birth on sacred stones to give their children power. Stones lie in a grove of trees with pineapple fields all

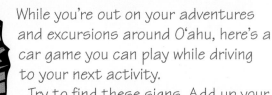

Sign Hunt

While you're out on your adventures and excursions around O'ahu, here's a car game you can play while driving to your next activity.

Try to find these signs. Add up your points at the end. Anyone can play and any number of kids can join. Whoever sees the sign first receives the points. They could be anywhere on the island, so keep your eyes peeled! Good luck.

A. (3 points)

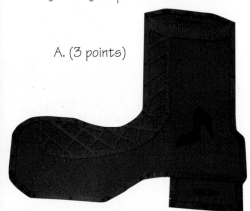

B. (5 points)

C. (3 points)

D. (3 points)

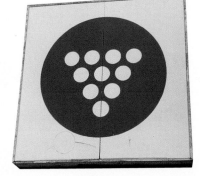

E. (7 points)

around. At the intersection of Whitmore Avenue and Kamehameha Highway in Wahiawā. **FREE**

Wizard Stones of Waikīkī
These four enormous boulders were brought to Waikīkī by four great kāhuna (wizards) from Tahiti. They were once used in Hawaiian healing rituals, and are still said to contain great powers. Located on Kūhiō Beach in Waikīkī, surrounded by an iron fence for protection. **FREE**

Healing Stones of Wahiawā
Peek inside of the small shrine and you will see sacred Hawaiian healing stones. They were once famous in the Hawaiian Islands, but now few people come to visit them. Located on California Avenue in Wahiawā, a mile west of Kamehameha Highway, on the corner of Ka'alalo Place, between the Methodist Church and elementary school. **FREE**

Cultural Learning Center at Ka'ala
Native Hawaiian values, cultural practices, and farming are taught through workshops in poi pounding, taro planting, lauhala weaving and other science and culture workshops. Open for guided tours and workshops by request only; call ahead to schedule. 85-555 Farrington Highway in Wai'anae • Ph: 696-9411

Mauka Makai Excursions (PR)
Hike to Hawaiian archeological sites including heiaus (temples), ko'a (fishing shrines), and petroglyphs (rock carvings). Half- or full-day adventures will take your family through tropical rainforests and along coastal areas to learn about O'ahu's legends and history. Kids

Try look!
(it's a car game for kids)

While you're in the car, going to the zoo or aquarium, see who can find these things. Whoever finds it first gets the points.

A one-way sign	1 point
A kid on skates	3 points
A person walking a dog	5 points
A man jogging with headphones on	8 points

ages 6–17 must be accompanied by parent. Full day is $63 for kids (6–17), $78 for adults; half day is $32 for kids, $46 for adults. www.oahu-ecotours.com • Ph: 593-3525

Historic Hawai'i

Learn about the history of Hawai'i after the arrival of Captain Cook in 1778. At these places you'll see what the islands were like in the old days of whale hunting, missionaries, sugar and pineapple plantations, Chinatown, and World War II. You'll also learn about the many ethnic groups that settled in Hawai'i and the history of surfing.

Hawai'i Plantation Village

You can walk through eight different villages and learn how Hawai'i's early plantation workers lived a hundred years ago. Check out the exciting Plantation Heritage Festival in September. Guided tours Monday

The Okinawan house is one of the many houses you can see at Hawai'i's Plantation Village. Step back in time and see Hawai'i the way it was. Photo courtesy of Hawai'i Plantation Village.

through Saturday. **FREE** to kids 5 and under; kids 5–12, $3; college students with ID and seniors, $4; kama'aina and military, $5; adults, $7. 94-695 Waipahu Street at Waipahu Cultural Garden Park • www.hawaii plantationvillage.org • Ph: 677-0110

Tucked away from the main road is the 'Ewa Beach Railway. See old trains and take a ride back in time.

'Ewa Beach Railway

A hundred years ago, trains carried people and cargo all around the island. Learn about Hawai'i's railroads at the **FREE** museum and take a 13-mile ride on a little plantation-era train. Train rides on Sundays at 12:30 and 2:30 p.m.; cost is $5 for kids 2–12; $8 for adults. 91-1001 Renton Road in 'Ewa • Ph: 681-5461

Bishop Museum

One of the best places on the island to learn about Hawai'i's history. Walk under a gigantic whale skeleton as you look at real weapons, drums, capes, and other objects from ancient Hawai'i and Polynesia. You'll also learn about the different groups that came to Hawai'i to work on the plantations and see their colorful traditional costumes. Check out the big-screen shows at the Planetarium and live hula performances everyday at 11 a.m. and 2 p.m. Don't miss the Hawai'i Sports Hall of Fame. **FREE** for kids 3 and under; kids ages 4–12 and seniors, $12; adults, $15. Special rates for kama'aina with ID. 1525 Bernice Street • www.bishopmuseum.org • Ph: 847-3511

The *Falls of Clyde* is only one of the features at the Hawai'i Maritime Center.

Mission Houses Museum

Step back in time as you walk through houses built for the missionaries almost 200 years ago! They traveled by ship all the way to Hawai'i to teach the Hawaiians about their God. Take a tour of three real missionary homes and learn how they churned butter by hand and printed their own books. Open Tuesday through Saturday. Daily tours are **FREE** for kids 5 and under; $6 for kids 6 and up; $8 for kama'aina with ID, military, and seniors; $10 for adults. 553 South King Stree • www.lava.net/~mhm/ • Ph: 531-0481

Hawai'i Maritime Center and the Falls of Clyde

If you like boats, you'll love the Hawai'i Maritime Center. Check out the skeleton of a humpback whale and walk through hands-on exhibits about Hawai'i's ocean environment and whaling history. Step aboard the historic *Falls of Clyde,* a four-masted sailing ship built in 1878, and the *Hokule'a,* a double-hulled sailing canoe built just like canoes from Hawai'i's past. Located at Pier 7 on Honolulu Harbor. Kids 6 and under **FREE**; ages 6–17, $4.50; adults, $7.50. www.bishopmuseum.org/hmc • Ph: 536-6373

North Shore Surf and Cultural Museum

Learn all about the history of surfing on Oʻahu's famous North Shore. Check out some cool antique surfboards, the first snowboard, and watch surf movies all day. Open most afternoons in Waialua's North Shore Marketplace. **FREE** www.captainrick.com/surf_museum.htm • Ph: 637-8888

Honolulu Timewalks

Travel back in time on fun, historical walking tours of the city. Guides dress in old-fashioned costumes and let you in on the hidden secrets of Honolulu's past. At least twenty different tours with names like "Haunted Honolulu" and "The Revolution of 1893." Tours are scheduled throughout the year, call ahead for reservations. 2634 South King Street #3 • Ph: 943-0371

Waikīkī Historic Trail

Families can take a trip into Waikīkī's exciting past on this self-guided walking tour. See where Hawaiian kings and queens had their homes, pass by the magical Wizard Stones, and stand in the royal coconut grove first planted by a chief more than 400 years ago! **FREE** guided tours Monday through Saturday at 9 a.m. Meet at Royal Hawaiian Shopping Center in Waikīkī. www.waikikihistorictrail.com • Ph: 737-6442

Aloha Tower

Climb ten stories (or take the elevator!) to the top of Aloha Tower, built in 1926 as a symbol of aloha to greet visitors arriving by ship. After you've checked out the views, have lunch at Aloha Tower Marketplace. **FREE** At Honolulu Harbor next to the Hawaiʻi Maritime Center •

There's a lot of fun stores at the Aloha Tower Marketplace.

HAWAIIAN LANGUAGE 202

ACROSS

3. honorable, magnificent, noble, stately
6. water
7. family
8. porch, veranda
9. Christmas
15. ocean
16. crooked, out of shape (an Oʻahu town west of Pearl Harbor)
17. house
18. tapa

DOWN

1. woman
2. born in Hawaiʻi (local)
4. _____ chicken (rotisserie)
5. delicious
10. grandparent, ancestor
11. lizard
12. man
13. foster child, adopted child
14. bird

Get lost in the "World's Largest Maze" at Dole Plantation. With nearly two miles of paths lined by colorful Hawaiian plants, this is an amazing adventure! PHOTO COURTESY OF DOLE PLANTATION.

www.alohatower.com/ tower_index.htm • Ph: 528-5700

Dole Pineapple Plantation and Maze

Ever wonder where Hawaiian pineapples come from? Take a ride on the Dole Pineapple Express train and find out. You can find your way through the world's largest Pineapple Garden Maze and walk through a Plantation Garden to see what coffee, chocolate, and banana plants look like. At the end of your journey, stop into the Dole Pineapple Pavilion to taste fresh pineapple slices and gulp down some pineapple juice. Visiting Dole Plantation is **FREE**. The Pineapple Express costs $5.50 for kids; $7.50 for adults. The Maze costs $3 for kids; $5 for adults. 64-1550 Kamehameha Highway in Wahiawā • www.dole-plantation. com • Ph: 621-8408

Punchbowl Crater/National Memorial Cemetery of the Pacific

This famous cemetery, set inside of an ancient volcanic crater, honors soldiers killed in battles across the Pacific. Visit on a holiday like Veteran's Day, Memorial Day, or Pearl Harbor Day (on December 7) and you'll see the cemetery covered with thousands of colorful leis. **FREE** 2177 Pūowaina Drive in Honolulu • Ph: 532-3720

Chinatown

Watch the lion dance, eat dim sum and fortune cookies, and make offerings at a Buddhist temple in Honolulu's Chinatown. The whole family can

take a guided walking tour to learn about hidden and historic places. Tours are offered by the Hawai'i Heritage Center (521-2749), Chinese Chamber of Commerce (533-3181), The Haunt (943-0371). In downtown Honolulu between Nimitz Highway, River Street, Vineyard Boulevard, and Bethel Street • www.chinatownhi.com

'Iolani Palace (PR)

King Kalākaua and Queen Kapi'olani once lived here in the only royal palace that exists in the United States. Take a grand tour of the Throne Room and the bedrooms where the king and queen slept. Fridays at noon you can picnic on the lawn while the Royal Hawaiian Band plays a **FREE** concert. Check out the famous statue of King Kamehameha across King Street in front of Ali'iolani Hale, home of the State Supreme Court.

Open Tuesday through Saturday. Call ahead for tours (kids must be 5 and older), which cost $5 for kids 5–17; $15 for kama'aina adults; $20 for adults.

Once a month on "Kama'aina Sunday" Hawai'i residents with ID can take the tour for **FREE**. On the corner of King and Richards streets in downtown Honolulu • www.iolanipalace.org • Ph; 522-0832/522-0823

Kawaiaha'o Church

Check out Hawai'i's most famous church, built from huge blocks cut by hand from the coral reef in 1842. Don't miss the outdoor fountain and the cemetery where Hawaiian kings are buried beside famous missionaries. **FREE** tours are offered on weekdays, and services in Hawaiian and English every Sunday at 8 a.m. and 10:30 a.m. 957 Punchbowl Street on the corner of King Street. • Ph: 522-1333

USS *Arizona* Memorial

O'ahu's Pearl Harbor became famous around the world in 1941 when Japanese planes dropped bombs on American military ships and sank

'Iolani Palace

Kawaiaha'o Church.

the USS *Arizona* battleship here. You can see it all for yourself at the USS *Arizona* Memorial. Look over the edge into the water where the sunken ship still lies and you'll see drops of oil bubbling to the surface from the ship's fuel tank. Located on the shore of Pearl Harbor off Kamehameha Highway (99) at 1 *Arizona* Memorial Place. No bathing suits or bare feet. Children under 5 must be accompanied by an adult. **FREE** www.arizonamemorial.org • Ph: 422-0561

USS *Bowfin* Submarine

Have you ever walked inside a real Navy submarine? Check out the USS *Bowfin,* a World War II sub based in Pearl Harbor. You can explore the submarine's crew quarters below deck, then visit the submarine museum next door where you'll find a C-3 submarine missile, submarine models and battleflags, and photos and posters from World War II. Admission is $3 for kids 4–12; $6 for kama'aina with ID; $8 for adults. Kids under 4 can visit the museum but can't go on board the sub. Located next to the Arizona Memorial—take the exit off Kamehameha Highway (99) to the Arizona Memorial and follow the signs to the *Bowfin*. www.bowfin.org • Ph: 423-1341

Battleship *Missouri*

On the deck of this battleship, known as the "Mighty Mo," the Japanese finally surrendered in 1945, bringing World War II to an end. You can step back in time and explore the many levels of this famous battleship—from the captain's cabin to the combat center and the machinery rooms down below. General admission is $8 for kids and $16 for adults. Four different guided tours are offered for varying prices; some are age restricted. Call ahead for details and reservations. Located at Ford Island in Pearl Harbor; park and buy tickets at the Bowfin Museum. www.ussmissouri.com • Ph: 973-2494

Home of the Brave

Curious about what really happened on the "Day of Infamy" and want to learn more than what the USS *Arizona* Memorial has to offer? Take the Home of the Brave tour and listen to an experienced guide dressed in a WWII Army Air Corps uniform as he transports you back in time to the 1940s. Known as the most comprehensive and exclusive tour of its kind in Hawai'i, guests visit the USS *Arizona* Memorial, Wheeler Army Airfield, Schofield Army Barracks, Fort Shafter, and Punchbowl National Memorial to see all the sites that were intimately affected by December 7, 1941. Contact them for more information regarding tour times and fees. www.pearlharborhq.com • Ph: 396-8112

Queen Emma's Summer Palace

When Honolulu got too hot during the summer, Queen Emma and King Kamehameha IV came here, to their palace in cool Nu'uanu. You can see where the king and queen slept and walk through their gardens. After visiting the palace, have lunch in the park next door under the huge ban-

Kids try on army uniforms after taking the Home of the Brave tour at the exclusive Home of the Brave museum. PHOTO COURTESY OF HOME OF THE BRAVE.

Queen Emma's Summer Palace.

yan tree. Admission is $1 for kids under 15; $4 for seniors and kama'aina; and $5 for adults. 2139 Pali Highway • www.daughtersofhawaii.org/hanaiakamalama/index.shtml • Ph: 595-3167

Byodo-in Temple at Valley of the Temples Memorial Park

The magnificent Byodo-in Buddhist temple was built in honor of the first wave of Japanese immigrants to arrive in Hawai'i. After making an offering, anyone can ring the gigantic 3-ton brass Peace Bell. The loud bong can be heard all across the park. As peacocks wander

Practice the lotus position at the Byodo-In Temple and experience a moment of serenity.

Feel like meditating? Go to the Byodo-in Temple—its beautiful surroundings are worth the trip.

by with their tails spread wide, kids can stand on a bridge above the huge fishpond and feed the very hungry koi fish with pellets bought at the gift shop. Take off your shoes before you enter the temple where a 9-foot-tall Buddha meditates peacefully. Admission is $2 per person. Snacks sold in the gift shop. 47-200 Kahekili Highway in Kāneʻohe. Drive to the back of Valley of the Temples Memorial Park. • Ph: 239-8811

US Army Museum
Get a close-up look at the military tanks that line the sidewalk outside the US Army Museum, then venture upstairs to see a massive gun and a real army helicopter that has set down on

See the many exhibits at the US Army Museum. PHOTO COURTESY OF THE US ARMY MUSEUM.

the roof. Inside, you'll feel like you're part of a top secret mission as you make your way through the underground hallways of what used to be a US Army defense post. Travel through exhibits on Hawaiian warfare, the Pearl Harbor attack, then jump across a make-believe booby trap in the floor and come face to face with camouflaged guerilla fighters as you enter the exhibits on Vietnam and Korea. On the corner of Saratoga and Kalia Road in Waikīkī, park in the lot next to Fort DeRussy. **FREE** www.leahi.net/hams/museum/ • Ph: 955-9552

Damien Museum

This small museum gives you a peek into the life of Father Damien, a Belgian priest who came to Hawai'i to help the people with Hansen's disease (leprosy) who lived in exile at Kalaupapa on Moloka'i. Step into St. Augustus Church and see the beautiful stained glass windows. **FREE** Closed on weekends. 130 Ōhua Avenue behind St. Augustus Church in Waikīkī • Ph: 923-2690

Tropic Lightning Museum

Learn about Hawai'i's own "Tropic Lightning" division of the US Army, men and women who fought in World War II and in Vietnam and Korea. Closed Sundays and Mondays. **FREE** Building 361 Wai'anae Avenue in Schofield Barracks • Ph: 655-0438

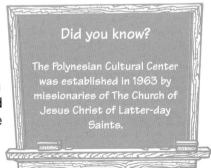

Did you know?

The Polynesian Cultural Center was established in 1963 by missionaries of The Church of Jesus Christ of Latter-day Saints.

Polynesian Cultural Center

Explore seven Polynesian villages, each one from a different island group: Hawai'i, Fiji, New Zealand, Tahiti, Samoa, the Marquesas, and Tonga. At each village the whole family can taste food from different cultures and learn songs, dances, and crafts. Kids can play games like Samoan "pick-up sticks," Tahitian checkers, and poi balls. Stay after sunset for the lū'au and exciting Polynesian night show with chanting, dancing, and fire walking. Closed Sundays. Kids 5 and under **FREE**; kids 5–11, $16; $27 for adults. Evening show and lū'au cost extra. 55-370 Kamehameha Highway in Lā'ie • www.polynesia.com • Ph: 293-3000

Try look!
(it's a car game for kids)

While you're in the car, going to your next adventure, see who can find these things. Whoever finds it first gets the points.

A pedestrian crossing sign	1 point
An orange traffic cone	3 points
The word Hawai'i	5 points
A Garage Sale sign	8 points

Waikīkī Trolley

The whole family will enjoy rides on these open-air trolleys that cover the whole island—not just Waikīkī! Trolley tours take you around historic Honolulu and Chinatown, down the south shore to Hālona Blowhole and Sea Life Park, to the best shopping and dining on the island, even out to Waikele. A fun and convenient way to get around O'ahu while taking in the sights. All-day pass for kids 4–11 is $10; teens 12–18, $14; adults, $20. Discounts offered on their website. Buy tickets at: www.waikikitrolley.com • Ph: 593-2822

Waimea Valley Adventure Park

See how the Native Hawaiians lived off the land in Waimea Valley on the North Shore. Watch cliff-divers plunge into pools, play Ha-

Waimea Falls Park is a great place to spend the day with family. PHOTO COURTESY OF ATLANTIS ADVENTURES.

waiian games, and learn about the Hawaiian language and hula. A keiki play area and Jungle Treks for kids make it fun for little ones. Guided hikes, horseback riding, mountain biking trails, and ATV tours are exciting for older kids and parents. Admission is $12 for kids 4–12; $24 for adults. Be sure to call first to make sure the park is open. 59-864 Kamehameha Highway • Ph: 955-TARO (8276)

More Tours and Adventures

There's lots to do around O'ahu if you just want to have some plain old fun—no history lessons attached. Try your toes on ice skates at the Ice Palace or take a glider tour way up in the clouds. There's horseback riding and submarine tours, swimming with dolphins and water slides, the list goes on and on.

Submarine Rides (PR)

Dive down 100 feet to the ocean floor without even getting your feet wet! See sunken ships, coral reefs, and more marine life than you can count on both hands and feet. Call ahead for reservations.

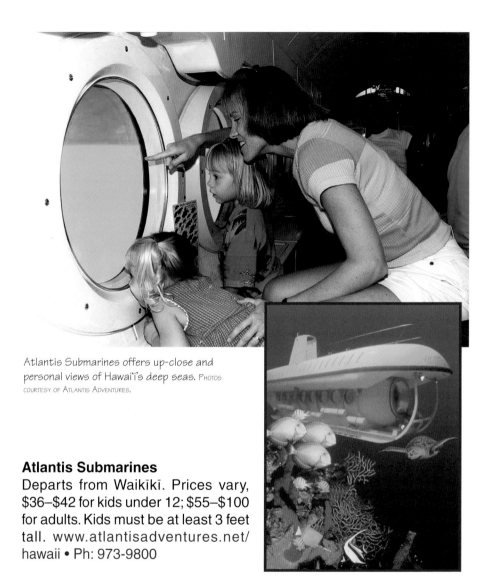

Atlantis Submarines offers up-close and personal views of Hawai'i's deep seas. PHOTOS COURTESY OF ATLANTIS ADVENTURES.

Atlantis Submarines

Departs from Waikīkī. Prices vary, $36–$42 for kids under 12; $55–$100 for adults. Kids must be at least 3 feet tall. www.atlantisadventures.net/hawaii • Ph: 973-9800

Nautilus

Semi-sub goes only halfway underwater, but lower cabin with windows is fully submerged. Kids 3 and under **FREE**; $39 for kids 4–11; $59 for adults. All ages welcome. • Ph: 239-9110

Pacific Splash Cruises

Cruise along the Diamond Head coastline, then strap on your mask and fins, slip down the giant water slide into the ocean, and jump on a floating trampoline. Brunch, BBQ lunch, and dinner cruises available. Dolphin- and whale-watching tours also offered. Kids 4–12, $20–$40; adults, $30–$70. Call for reservations. www.dreamcruises.com • Ph: 592-5200

Dolphin- and Whale-Watching Adventures

Get up close to humongous humpback whales, and if you're feeling brave, jump in the water and swim with friendly spinner dolphins!

Dolphin Excursions

Offers exciting whale-watching tours from January to March only, dolphin snorkeling tours are available April to December. $45–55 for kids 4–12, $70-$95 for adults. www.dolphinexcursions.com • Ph: 239-5579 (PR)

Dolphin QUEST

A dolphin-training program at the Kahala Mandarin Hotel. Kids 5–12 can swim with dolphins in a saltwater pool and learn to feed and play games with them. $150 for kids 5–12, two-hour session; $175 13 and up and adults, one hour. (PD) Kāhala Mandarin Oriental; 5000 Kāhala Avenue • www.dolphinquest.org • Ph: 739-8918

Skate, Slide, Ride, Glide

Ice Palace

Ice skating in Hawai'i? You bet. Cool off with your friends and family at the ice rink in Salt Lake. The youth ice hockey league runs year-round for all age groups—from the Squirts (age 9 and under) to the Juniors (18–20). The whole family can sign up for skate school and learn to figure-skate like pros. You can even have your birthday party on the ice! Admission is $6.50 per person; skate school and ice hockey cost extra. 4510 Salt Lake Boulevard • www.icepalacehawaii.com • Ph: 487-9921/488-3037

Sure, the beach is fun, but these rides can't be beat. PHOTO COURTESY OF HAWAIIAN WATERS ADVENTURE PARK.

Hawaiian Waters Adventure Park

Wet and wild fun for everyone in the family! Walk across giant lily pads and float down an 800-foot river. Then race your friends down the slippery side of a volcano, and check out the world's wildest water half-pipe. Little ones will love the Keiki Cove's mini-slides, waterfalls, and water cannons. Adults can hang at the Island bar and whirlpool spa. You can even have your birthday party here!

Admission for kids 4–11, $22; adults, $33; seniors 60 and up, $15. Special discounts for kamaʻaina with ID. Days and hours depend on the season, call ahead to find out. 400 Farrington Highway in Kapolei • www.hawaiianwaters.com • Ph: 945-3928/ 674-9283

Just for laughs

Why do birds fly south?

Because it's too far to walk.

Happy Trails Hawai'i Horseback Riding Adventures

The whole family can saddle up and ride the country trails of the North Shore. Kids 6 and up only. Call ahead for prices and reservations. 59-231 Pūpūkea Road on the North Shore • www.happytrailshawaii.com • Ph: 638-7433

Other horseback riding adventures (call ahead for prices and schedules):
Kualoa Ranch (ages 3 and up): 237-8515
Turtle Bay Resort: 293-8811
Waimea Valley Adventure Park: 955-TARO

Horseback Riding Lessons:

Kualoa Ranch: 237-8515
New Town & Country Stables: 259-9941
Whispering Hills Training Farm: 668-6540
Koko Crater Equestrian Center: 395-2628

Glider Rides (PR)

Go for a wild ride in the clouds with Mom or Dad on a glider plane. You'll feel like a bird as you drift on the wind, or turn and somersault in the air. All ages with a parent, kids must be at least 11 to fly without an adult. $40–70 for 15–30 minute flights. Flights for 1–2 people only leave from Dillingham Airfield on the North Shore. Call ahead for reservations. Dillingham Airfield, Route 930 in Mokulē'ia • www.soarhawaii.com • Ph: 677-3404

Fun Idea!

How well do you know O'ahu? Play the game "Mauka or Makai?" while out on your next adventure. Designate a map person (use the map in this book or a Hawai'i atlas) to call out places on the island. Players have to guess whether the place called out is mauka or makai of their destination.

GO TAKE A HIKE

Have you ever hiked into an ancient volcanic crater? Have you walked down the abandoned Old Pali Road, now overgrown with ginger and guava trees? There are hundreds of hikes on Oʻahu that are fun for the whole family—so put on your hiking shoes and let's go!

PARENTS: People are lost hiking on Oʻahu every year, so be careful. Don't let kids hike alone. When you go, always tell someone where you're going. Bring water, sunscreen, mosquito repellent, snacks, and athletic shoes. Cell phones are helpful in case you get lost. Always stay on the trail and don't drink from streams—Hawaiʻi's streams are known to have harmful bacteria that will make you sick. Hikes in this section are graded in two levels of difficulty for kids from beginner to intermediate. For more detailed descriptions, see Stuart Ball's *Hiker's Guide to Oʻahu* book.

Makapuʻu Lighthouse
Easy, paved trail uphill to the Makapuʻu Lighthouse. You might see humpback whales spouting from the top. It can get hot during mid-day, so bring water. Dogs and baby strollers can go too!
Start: Park on the side of Kalanianaʻole Highway right after you pass the Hawaiʻi Kai Golf Course (heading towards Waimānalo from town). Enter the trail at the black gate on the ocean side of the highway and follow the paved path up the side of the hill, then around to the left until you reach the Lighthouse. Return the way you came.
Length: about 3 miles round trip
Level: Beginner

Take a family hike down Old Pali Road and experience old Hawai'i.

Old Pali Road

This short, paved hike starts at the Nuʻuanu Pali Lookout and takes you down the old Pali highway that was built in 1897. It is paved, although it can get

slippery when wet. Nice views of the windward side, and sweet-smelling yellow ginger along the way. Stroller-friendly.

Start: Park at the Pali Lookout (follow the signs from the Pali Highway in both directions). Don't leave valuables in the

Safety First!

Hiking is a great way to spend the day with your family—everyone gets some exercise while exploring Hawai'i's beautiful landscape up close. But, of course, it's always important to be prepared and safe. Here are a few safety tips compiled from the American Red Cross website and the Hawaii Department of Land and Natural Resources:

Hiking safety
- Practice sun safety (see page 8).
- Always tell someone where you are going and when you plan on returning.
- Allow plenty of time for the hike—the last thing you want is to try and find your way down a trail in the dark. Figure on 1.5 miles per hour. Start your hike early in the day.
- Be aware of the terrain you'll be hiking, weather conditions and hazards along the trail. Be prepared for a change of weather: take raincoats and towels.
- Bring supplies you might need: a first aid kit, a cell phone, lots of water, and snacks—especially for younger children.
- Don't rush your kids. Let them explore naturally. The hike should be about seeing new things, not getting to the end of the trail and back. Even the youngest of children can be taken on a hike: they may not finish the full length of the hike, but that's okay.
- Wear proper clothing—you need protection from the sun, insects, wind or rain—and proper shoes! Slippers are great most of the time, but aren't good for hiking.
- Always stay on the designated trail. Leaving the trail may get you lost and may cause damage to Hawai'i's flora and fauna.
- Hike in groups and keep track of everyone. Don't let children stray too far.
- Never drink from Hawai'i's streams. If your child has open cuts, make sure they are covered completely before wading through water.
- Be aware of any postings before beginning the hike: there are some trails that are open to hunting during certain times of the year. Contact the Department of Land and Natural Resources for information.
- And always respect the 'āina. Don't leave trash, destroy any of the landscape or take anything. Hawai'i's trails should be enjoyed for future generations.

car. Head down to the right from the lookout and follow the road through the big, black gate. About two-thirds of the way down, you'll come to a rock wall and a palm tree. This is a good place to stop for snacks. More adventurous hikers can climb over the wall and trek up this mini-valley until it ends at a small waterfall. From the rock wall, you can head back up or continue down the paved highway until it ends at the current Pali Highway.

Length: about 1 mile round trip (not including a side-hike up the valley)
Level: Beginner

Mānoa Falls

A popular hike in the back of Mānoa Valley that takes you to a small waterfall. It can get muddy after a rain shower, so wear shoes and clothes you don't mind getting dirty. The trail is well-maintained with bamboo groves, big trees and follows a stream. It ends at a viewing deck of the waterfall.

The start of the trail to Mānoa Falls.

Start: The trail begins past the entrances to former Paradise Park and Lyon Arboretum at the end of Mānoa Road. Don't leave valuables in the car.

Length: 1.6 miles round trip

Level: Beginner

Maunawili Trail (or the "Hairpin Turn Trail")

This trail will take you along the base of the Koʻolaus in the very back of Maunawili. It is an easy, level hike with beautiful views of the mountains (above you) and the windward side. Follow it for as long as you like. The trail goes on for 10 miles and eventually ends in Waimānalo. Kids will probably want to go only part of the way.

Start: Take the Pali Highway going Kailua-bound and pull off at the scenic lookout at the hairpin turn (before the intersection with Kamehameha Highway). Walk up to the right of the lookout parking lot and go through the guardrail. Follow the trail up the steps and to the left. You'll see a sign for Maunawili Trail here. Pass the water tank and continue along the trail for as long as you choose. Turn back and return the way you came.

Length: up to 10 miles one way; make it as short or long as you like

Level: Beginner

Just for laughs

What has 50 legs but can't walk?

Half a centipede.

Kuliʻouʻou Valley Hike

A quiet, shady hike into Kuliʻouʻou Valley that passes through kukui groves and ends with two waterfalls. Follow Kuliʻouʻou Road as it winds back into the valley. Turn right on Kalaʻau Place. Park just before the dead-end circle. Climb over the chain and follow the one-lane road back into the valley to the Kuliʻouʻou Valley Trail. Return the way you came.

Length: 2 miles round trip

Level: Beginner

Hiking

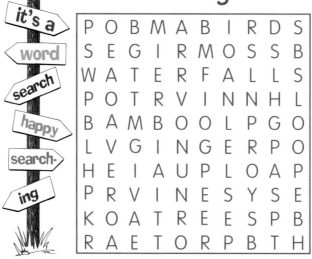

it's a word search happy search-ing

P	O	B	M	A	B	I	R	D	S
S	E	G	I	R	M	O	S	S	B
W	A	T	E	R	F	A	L	L	S
P	O	T	R	V	I	N	N	H	L
B	A	M	B	O	O	L	P	G	O
L	V	G	I	N	G	E	R	P	O
H	E	I	A	U	P	L	O	A	P
P	R	V	I	N	E	S	Y	S	E
K	O	A	T	R	E	E	S	P	B
R	A	E	T	O	R	P	B	T	H

Try to find all these things you might discover on your hike. Some are horizontal, vertical, diagonal, and backwards. Circle the ones you find.

petroglyph	mango
waterfalls	heiau
ginger	pools
birds	protea
bamboo	moss
koa trees	vines

Maunawili Falls Trail

A popular valley hike that follows Maunawili Stream to a waterfall and deep swimming hole. An easy hike, but it can be muddy and crowded on weekends.

Start: Park on Kelewina Street (off Maunawili Road) and walk down to the one-lane private road. Follow the road until the sign for Maunawili Falls Trail on the right; the trail goes uphill and into the valley until you reach the waterfall and pool. The trail is well-maintained and easy to follow. Return the way you came.

Length: 3 miles round trip

Level: Beginner to Intermediate

Judd Trail

This short loop trail will take you through groves of bamboo, eucalyptus and Norfolk pine trees. On the way back you'll pass Jackass Ginger, a

popular swimming hole—so bring your bathing suit! The trail can be muddy and don't forget your mosquito repellent. Stay on the main trail; it's easy to get side-tracked.

Start: Park on Nu'uanu Pali Road on the side of the road past the trail entrance (you'll see concrete barriers on the side of the road just before a small bridge). Don't leave valuables in the car. Walk into the trail entrance

Sunlight streams through the trees at the beginning of Judd Trail.

Sign Hunt

While you're out on your adventures and excursions around Oʻahu, here's a car game you can play while driving to your next activity.

Try to find these signs. Add up your points at the end. Anyone can play and any number of kids can join. Whoever sees the sign first receives the points. They could be anywhere on the island, so keep your eyes peeled! Good luck.

A. (3 points)

B. (3 points)

C. (5 points)

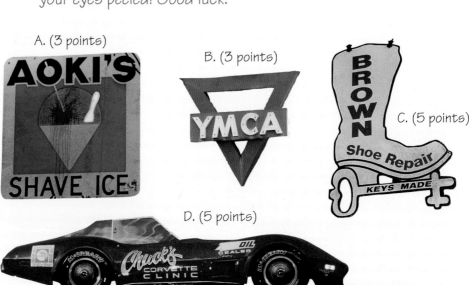

D. (5 points)

E. (7 points)

F. (5 points)

G. (7 points)

and down to Nuʻuanu Stream. Cross it here and go straight at the sign for the Judd Trail. Stay on the main Judd Trail as it weaves to the right, then downhill towards the stream. To swim in Jackass Ginger pool, follow the dirt trail downhill to the stream after passing the metal stake. Climb back up to the main trail after your swim, and follow it upstream to where you started.
Length: 3/4-mile loop
Level: Beginner to Intermediate

Puʻu Pia Trail
A short uphill hike at the back of Mānoa Valley that ends at a bench with great views of Mānoa and Honolulu. Have a picnic lunch on the grassy hill at the end of the hike.
Start: Park on Alani Drive just before the intersection with Woodlawn Drive. Walk down one-lane Alani Drive past houses until it turns into a dirt path. Climb over a wire blocking the path, stay left on the Puʻu Pia Trail. Return the way you came.
Length: 2 miles round trip
Level: Beginner to Intermediate

Diamond Head Crater
Climb to the top of this ancient volcanic crater and see all of the south shore below. The trail is hot and well-maintained, but there are lots of stairs and dark tunnels, so bring water and a flashlight!
Start: At the marked entrance to Diamond Head State Monument across from KCC on Diamond Head Road. Guided hikes of Diamond Head Crater are offered by the Clean Air Team—meet at 9 a.m. on Saturdays at the windsock in front of the Honolulu Zoo (948-3299).
Length: 1.4 miles round trip
Level: Beginner to Intermediate (lots of uphill steps)

Waimano Valley
This easy valley hike takes you through strawberry guava groves following a stream.
Start: Follow Moanalua Road until you reach Waimano Home Road, turn right. Drive

DIAMOND HEAD
STATE MONUMENT
DEPARTMENT
OF
LAND & NATURAL RESOURCES

into the Waimano Training School and Hospital and park in the dirt before the guard hut. Keep walking up Waimano Home Road. Follow the path to the left of the hunter mailbox and walk to the left of the chain-link fence. At the sign, go left on the lower Waimano Trail; you'll return from the upper trail.

Length: 2-mile loop
Level: Beginner to Intermediate

Makiki Loop Trail

This loop trail will take you uphill beside Kanealole Stream, over a short section of Makiki Valley Trail, then down the Maunalaha Ridge trail. You'll cross two streams and pass through a field of Job's tears, eucalyptus trees, Norfolk pines and taro patches.

Start: Park outside of the Hawai'i Nature Center at 2131 Makiki Heights Drive (take a right at the five mailboxes on the main road). The HNC has maps of all Makiki trails and restrooms. Walk past the Nature Center through the gate to Kanealole Trail. Walk uphill until you reach the end of Kanealole Trail at the sign under a kukui tree. Go right on the Makiki

'Aiea Loop Trail.

Valley Trail for 0.7 miles until you reach the four-way trail intersection. Go right on the Maunalaha Trail, a rocky and sometimes steep downhill trail, to return to the Hawai'i Nature Center. The Hawai'i Nature Center also offers guided family hikes on the Makiki Loop Trail for kids 7 and up (955-0100).
Length: 2.5 miles
Level: Intermediate

'Aiea Loop Trail
A popular shady 5-mile hike through the back of 'Aiea.
Start: Follow 'Aiea Heights Drive into the Keaīwa Heiau State Recreation Area. Park in the upper lot. Follow the sign to the 'Aiea Loop Trail.
Length: 5-mile loop
Level: Intermediate

Note:
Contact the Sierra Club for a listing of their family hikes. They have ongoing hikes, service projects and weekend trips throughout the year.
www.hi.sierraclub.org • Ph: 538-6616

Fun Idea!
Pretend you're an explorer while on your hike. Take binoculars, a compass, a sketch book, and a small voice recorder. Note where you go and what you see—draw plants and animals in your sketch book or make a map of where you hike; record the sounds of birds and your surroundings; pretend you're the first person ever to hike the path you're on. What do you see, hear, smell, feel?

LET'S GET CAMPY

Hawaiʻi is the perfect place to sleep under the stars. You can camp on the beach, go crab-hunting at night, and wake up to the sound of crashing waves. Or sleep surrounded by enormous plants, like explorers in a wild jungle. Oʻahu has lots of camping sites that are family friendly, the best sites for kids are listed below.

PARENTS: Camping permits are required to camp at Oʻahu's State and County campgrounds. Reservations and permits should be acquired in advance. Applications can be turned in at the offices listed. To find applications for State Park camping permits online, visit www.hawaii.gov/dlnr/dsp.

Bellows Field Beach Park
Beach camping among ironwood trees. Swimming, bodysurfing, and picnicking on military recreation base in Waimānalo. Open to the public only on weekends from noon on Friday to 8 a.m. Monday.
Location: 41-043 Kalanianaole Highway
Permit: Honolulu Department of Parks and Recreation (or any satellite City Hall)
650 South King Street • Ph: 523-4525

Waimānalo Beach Park
Beach camping in Waimānalo. Swimming, bodysurfing, and picnicking.
Location: 41-741 Kalanianaʻole Highway
Permit: Honolulu Department of Parks and Recreation (or any satellite

Safety First!

Hawai'i has such beautiful weather it's hard not to take advantage. Camping is a great way to spend time with family. Kids get to sleep in the great outdoors and get away from TVs, video games, DVDs and VCRs. You can talk story around the campfire, catch up with your kids' lives and relax under the stars. But of course, you have to be prepared. Here are a few safety tips compiled from the American Red Cross website:

Camping safety
- Make sure you have the proper permits necessary.
- Practice sun safety (see page 8).
- Practice water safety if you're camping by the beach (see page 8).
- Always tell someone where you are going and when you plan on returning.
- Make a checklist of all the things you will need before leaving. Try to think of any scenario. Always bring a first aid kit.
- Be aware of the terrain where you'll be setting up, weather conditons and any potential hazards.
- If you'll be camping in a secluded area, away from your vehicle, bring a radio with batteries so you can be upated on any weather changes.
- Make sure campfires are allowed in the area where you are camping. If you have a campfire, keep small children away and make sure the fire is out before going to bed. Mark the location so no one stumbles on hot embers in the dark.
- And always respect the 'āina. Don't leave trash, destroy any of the landscape or take anything.

Fun Idea!

What's a camp-out without smores and ghost stories around a campfire? If you're camping with friends and family, come up with an evening schedule of events—make smores, sing some songs (bring a guitar and an 'ukulele), and after the sun has set, get ready for some chickenskin!

WAIMANALO BEACH PARK
PICNIC AND CAMP AREA NO.1
DEPARTMENT OF PARKS & RECREATION
CITY AND COUNTY OF HONOLULU

City Hall)
650 South King Street •
Ph: 523-4525

Waimānalo Beach Park is a great place for camping.

Hoʻomaluhia Botanical Garden
Camping on weekends only in lush windward botanical garden. Hiking, fishing and picnicking. Call 233-7323 for night walks and fishing program.
45-680 Luluku Road
Permit: Required, and must be validated at the Visitor Center.
Honolulu Department of Parks and Recreation (or any satellite City Hall)
650 South King Street • Ph: 523-4525

Kualoa Beach Park
Camping on a big, grassy field next to the beach. Swimming and picnicking, activities like horseback riding and kayaking offered through Kualoa Ranch (237-7321).
Location: 49-479 Kamehameha Hwy
Permit: Honolulu Department of Parks and Recreation (or any satellite City Hall)
650 South King Street • Ph: 523-4525

Kahana Valley State Park
Camping in lush Kahana Valley across from the beach and a historic fishpond. Swimming, hiking, fishing, picnicking and pig hunting.
Location: 52-222 Kamehameha Highway
Permit: Hawaiʻi State Parks
1151 Punchbowl Street, Rm 131 • Ph: 587-0300

Mālaekahana State Recreation Area
Campsites and cabins at beach park surrounded by ironwood trees. Camping, swimming, snorkeling, bodysurfing, beachcombing, picnicking, and trips to Goat Island. Kahuku section has cabins and **FREE** camping

Waimānalo Beach Park

DA KINE PIDGIN

ACROSS

1. What you get when you feel an obake in the room.
5. "Them"
6. "That"
7. A word that can be used for anything. (hint: The title of this crossword.)
8. Big. Really big.
11. Crazy, stupid-head.
12. Stingy.
13. A smelly odor (fart).

DOWN

2. Gotta wipe this off your face with a tissue (or sea water).
3. Okay then.
4. Don't show off.
8. "_____ da mouth," is something you say when your plate lunch is so ono.
9. Sometime, soon enough.
10. Hello. How are you?
11. Like that.

(no permit required)—contact Friends of Mālaekahana at 293-1736. Kalanai Point section is run by State Parks, permit required.
Location: Off Kamehameha Highway between Lāʻie and Kahuku.
Permit: Hawaiʻi State Parks
1151 Punchbowl Street, Rm 131 • Ph: 587-0300

Keaīwa Heiau State Recreation Area
Forest camping near historic healing heiau in ʻAiea.
Location: End of ʻAiea Heights Drive
Permit: Hawaiʻi State Parks
1151 Punchbowl Street, Rm 131 • Ph: 587-0300

Sign up for Summer Camp

Mom and Dad don't want to go camping? Sign up for a summer camp. Spend a week or more with kids your own age, swimming, hiking, shooting bows and arrows and climbing through the treetops on exciting ropes courses. Or the whole family can roast marshmallows together at Camp Erdman's Family Camp!

Xtreme Adventure Camps by Kamaʻaina Kids
Learn to sail a three-masted schooner between the Hawaiian Islands. Spend a week surfing the North Shore. Sleep in cabins in the Waianae Mountains at Camp Timberline and climb the high ropes course. Or spend three weeks doing it all at the Hawaiian Adventure Combo Camp. Sessions run June through August for kids ages 10–17. Prices vary and kamaʻaina rates are available. Contact Kamaʻaina Kids for info about camps for younger kids.
www.kamaainakids.com • Ph: 262-4538

Spring Break Day Camps by Kamaʻaina Kids
Kids in grades K–6 can take a "Fantastic Voyage" around Oʻahu during Spring Break. Adventures include hiking, whale watching, horsemanship, visiting the zoo and going to the beach. Day camp is available from 6

a.m. to 6 p.m. the last two weeks of March. Locations all around O'ahu, $45 per day.
www.kamaainakids.com • Ph: 262-4538

SPIRIT Teen Spring Break Camp by Kama'aina Kids
Become part of a team as you climb the high ropes course and take on other team challenges. Spend four nights talking story under the stars with other kids your age. Four-night session at the end of March for kids 11–15. Drop-off and pick-up locations all around the island. Tuition is $250.
www.kamaainakids.com • Ph: 262-4538

Camp Erdman
This YMCA camp in Waialua offers weekend campout activities for groups

and families. Family Camp is for parents and kids of all ages with optional activities like archery, biking, ropes course, hikes, astronomy, and arts and crafts. Each family gets their own cabin. The Summer Resident Camp in Mokulē'ia for kids in grades 3–9 offers challenging and exciting activities while teaching lifelong skills. Horsemanship and surfing are also offered as upgrades.
69-385 Farrington Highway in Waialua; www.camperdman.net • Ph: 637-4615

Keiki build confidence during the ropes course at YMCA's Camp Erdman. PHOTO COURTESY OF THE YMCA OF HONOLULU.

E Komo Mai

An adventure camp for teens at Camp Erdman in Waialua. Campers spend 10 days during the summer swimming, snorkeling, hiking, boating, kayaking, surfing and learning Hawaiian arts, crafts, songs and dances. Activities take campers all around the island. Tuition is $1,500, including airfare from the mainland or outer island. Call for kamaʻaina rate.

69-385 Farrington Highway in Waialua; www.hawaiisummercamp.com • Ph: 676-9232/721-6841

Camp Mokulēʻia

Stay in cabins and spend the summer swimming and snorkeling, hiking, climbing ropes courses, building campfires, singing songs, and learning about Christian values in fun ways. Summer sessions at this Episcopal camp on the North Shore run from July to August. Kids from grades 3–12 can spend week-long sessions with others the same age. Cost is $300 for one week session, $550 for two weeks.

www.campmokuleia.org • Ph: 637-6241

Make new friends during a campout on the beach. PHOTO COURTESY OF THE YMCA OF HONOLULU.

KIDS ON WHEELS

If you don't want to walk somewhere, get on wheels and roll! There are tons of places to go on a skateboard, bike, scooter, rollerskates or blades.

PARENTS: While biking, skateboarding, or rollerblading, kids should always wear protective gear like kneepads, elbow pads and helmets. Most skateparks on O'ahu are unsupervised, and new skateparks are planned or in progress in Hale'iwa, Kapolei, Sunset Beach, Banzai Beach, Hau'ula, Pearl City and Waipahu. Go with your kids on bike rides. It'll be safer for them, and fun for everyone!

Skateparks

Public skateparks have been popping up all around O'ahu. Check out a park near you.

'A'ala Park
Plaza with banks, ledges and rails. **FREE**
280 North King Street • Ph: 522-7022

'Ewa Beach Skatepark
Funbox and spine ramps. **FREE**
91-955 North Road • Ph: 689-0370

Hickam Hangar Air Force Base Skatepark
Two-level bowl and mini-bowl. 50-50.com

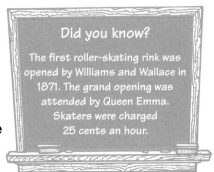

Did you know?

The first roller-skating rink was opened by Williams and Wallace in 1871. The grand opening was attended by Queen Emma. Skaters were charged 25 cents an hour.

says it has the "best wooden bowl ramps in the world!" $20 a year for membership plus $3 a day. $5 a day for non-members. Pads required. Must have military ID or military sponsor to get on base.
Ph: 448-4422

Kamiloiki Community Skatepark
Roller hockey rink and skatepark. **FREE**
7750 Hawai'i Kai Drive • Ph: 395-5314

Kāne'ohe Community Skatepark
Lots of ledges, 5-foot hip and a 3-foot funbox. **FREE**
45-660 Keaahala Road • Ph: 233-7308

Keolu Hills Skatepark
Large cement park with U-shaped bowls. **FREE**
1416 Keolu Drive in Kailua • Ph: 266-7818

Kamiloiki Community Skatepark.

Safety First!

Kids like to be on the go, and what faster way to go than on a set of wheels. But it's the parent's job to make sure they get there safely. There's one safety rule you need to enforce and repeat: helmet, helmet, helmet. Here are a few safety tips compiled from the National Safety Council and Lucile Packard Children's Hospital websites:

Skateboard safety
- Children 8 and under should have adult supervision while skateboarding.
- Before skateboarding, a parent should inspect the board for loose wheels, broken parts or cracks.
- Make sure your child wears safety gear: helmet, knee and elbow pads, and wrist braces. When buying a helmet, make sure it fits snugly and doesn't impede vision or hearing. The helmet should show as being approved by the American National Standards Institute, the American Society for Testing and Materials, the US Consumer Product Safety Commission. Talk to the store sales people: there are different types of helmets for different sports.
- Allow your child to choose the color of the helmet—he/she is more likely to wear it if they like it.
- Your child should wear closed shoes (not slippers).
- Road safety is especially important: skateboards should not be ridden in traffic or on busy sidewalks. Your child should know basic road rules.
- Teach your child to obey city laws and not to skate where it isn't permitted. There are lots of new skateparks around Oʻahu that are more fun than trying to skate on crowded sidewalks.
- Go with your kids to the skate parks. It's more fun than you might think.

Kamiloiki Community Skatepark.

Fun Idea!
Paint your helmet or decorate it with stickers to make it uniquely yours.

Makiki District Skatepark
Quarterpipes, ledges and half-pyramid. **FREE**
1527 Ke'eaumoku Street in Honolulu • Ph: 522-7082

Mililani District Skatepark
Cement park with ledges and mini-bowl. **FREE**
94-1150 Lanikuhana Avenue • Ph: 623-5258

Kamiloiki Community Skatepark.

Waianae Skatepark
Funboxes, ramps and jumps on blacktop court. **FREE**
Pililā'au District Park
85-166 Plantation Road • Ph: 696-4442

Bike Paths and Parks
There are many bike paths and bike-friendly parks on O'ahu that are fun for the whole family. Roller skates, blades, scooters and skateboards are also welcome.

Just for laughs

A kid returns to school after staying home sick.
The teacher asks, "Flu?"
The kid replies, "No, I rode my bike."

Lanikai Loop Bike Path
A nice ride beside the beach in Kailua. Mostly flat with one medium-sized hill. **FREE**
Start: At Kailua Beach Park on Kawailoa Road. Follow the bike path through the park, cross a bridge over the canal, then go up and over the hill into Lanikai. Watch out for cars and cross the road to 'A'alapapa Drive when it is safe. Stay in the

Sign Hunt

While you're out on your adventures and excursions around Oʻahu, here's a car game you can play while driving to your next activity.
Try to find these signs. Add up your points at the end. Anyone can play and any number of kids can join. Whoever sees the sign first receives the points. They could be anywhere on the island, so keep your eyes peeled! Good luck.

A. (3 points)

B. (5 points)

C. (5 points)

D. (3 points)

E. (4 points)

bike lane and follow Aʻalapapa Drive around the loop until it becomes Mokulua Drive. Return the way you came.
Length: 5-mile loop

Kawai Nui Marsh Bike Path
A peaceful ride through the Kawai Nui Marsh in Kailua. Ducks swim in the canal beside the paved path as you pedal towards Mount Olomana in the distance. Beautiful views of the marsh and Koʻolau Mountains.
Start: Park at Kawai Nui Neighborhood Park off Kīhāpai Street. Follow the path beside the wall to the end where it meets Kailua Road. Return the way you came.
Length: 2 miles round trip.

Date Street Bike Path
A flat ride through community gardens beside the Ala Wai canal and golf course. **FREE**
Start: Behind the Ala Wai Rec Center at McCully Street and Kapiʻolani

Start at Kailua Beach Park for a fantastic bike ride through the park over to Lanikai.

Safety First!

Kids like to be on the go, and what faster way to go than on a set of wheels. But it's the parent's job to make sure they get there safely. There's one safety rule you need to enforce and repeat: helmet, helmet, helmet. Here are a few safety tips compiled from the National Safety Council and Lucile Packard Children's Hospital websites:

Biking safety

- You child's bike should not be too big or complicated; the balls of his or her feet should be able to rest on the ground while seated.
- The bike should have a bell or horn in addition to reflectors in the front and back. Do not let young children ride after dark.
- Make sure your child wears safety gear: helmet, knee and elbow pads. When buying a helmet, make sure it fits snuggly and doesn't impede vision or hearing. The helmet should show as being approved by the American National Standards Institute, the American Society for Testing and Materials, the US Consumer Product Safety Commission. Talk to the store sales people: there are different types of helmets for different sports.
- Allow your child to choose the color of the helmet—he/she is more likely to wear it if they like it.
- Road safety is especially important. Your child should know basic road rules and how to cross the street safely.
- Go with your kids on a bike ride. It's more fun than you might think.

Boulevard. Follow the path along the Ala Wai Canal, then behind 'Iolani School. Turn right on Date Street, then go along the golf course and turn right on Kapahulu Avenue. Return the way you came.

Length: 2 miles round trip.

Kapiʻolani Park

A nice, flat ride around Kapiʻolani Park. May be crowded on weekends. **FREE**
Start: At the Honolulu Zoo entrance on Monsarrat and Kalākaua Avenues. Fol-

Did you know?

Kapiʻolani Park, named after Queen Kapiʻolani, was opened with a grand celebration by King Kalākaua on Kamehameha Day in 1877.

Kapiʻolani Park's bike path is perfect for any kid on wheels.

low the outside perimeter of the park down Monsarrat, turn right on Pākī
Avenue, then travel back down Kalākaua Avenue on the other side. Watch
out for walkers, joggers, rollerbladers, and people opening car doors.
Length: 2.1 miles

Sunset Beach Bike Path
A beautiful, flat bike ride beside the beach on the North Shore. **FREE**
Start: Just past Velzyland on the ocean side of Kamehameha Highway.
Follow the path to the Pūpūkea Foodland. Watch out for cars at intersec-
tions and driveways.
Length: 3.5 miles

Ala Moana Beach Park and Magic Island
Bike and jogging paths crisscross and circle this large, grassy beach
park. **FREE**
Across from Ala Moana Shopping Center at 1201 Ala Moana Boulevard.

Ala Moana Beach Park.

Kaka'ako Park is a great place for an end-of-day bike ride.

Kaka'ako Waterfront Park
Large coastal park with smooth hills and paved pathways that make this a great place to rollerskate or skateboard. **FREE**
End of 'Āhui and 'Ohe Streets off Ala Moana Boulevard.

Driving in Style

Driving isn't just for adults. Box car racing is fun and a great way to spend the weekend with family.

American Box Car Racing International
This nonprofit organization located in Pearl City offers a **FREE** Youth Volunteer Program where kids from 9–15 can join other kids every weekend (and Wednesdays) around the track. Learn how to build, tune and race box cars and help around the track. Snacks are provided for volunteers. Racing fees: $6 per person to watch or drive up to 4 hours; 4 and under—**FREE**; 55 & older—**FREE**. 25% discount for military families. They're open for parties! Currently located in Pearl City, plans are set to build a new facility in Kunia sometime in the future. For open racing times and additional information, contact 947-3393, Acacia Road, Pearl City (behind Sam's Club); www.boxcarracing.org • Ph: office, 947-3393, track, 454-9728

Wheels

it's a

word

search

happy

search-

ing

```
R A Z E R I C K H N H W
W O B I C Y C L E I W I
A E L C Y C I N U N H N
G L B L C Y C L E I E I
O S A I E I N G E R E R
N K O S A R I S L E L E
T A N D E M B I K E E T
L A B I A U Q L Y O Y O
T R I C Y C L E A O S O
Q B L A U D R I C D C C
I N L I N E S K A T E S
M O U N T A I N B I K E
```

Try to find all different modes of transportation with wheels. Some are horizontal, vertical, diagonal, and backwards. Circle the ones you find.

rollerblade

in-line skates

mountain bike

tandem bike

tricycle

razer

heeleys

scooter

wagon

bicycle

unicycle

For older kids: make a mousetrap car. Check out www.docfizzix.com to learn how. It's the most fun you'll have learning physics.

HANA HOU!
MUSIC & ENTERTAINMENT

Get out on the town and sample some of Oʻahu's culture. Movies on the big screen are fun, but check out the HUGE screen at the Imax and you'll be blown away. Go see a free hula show at Kūhiō Beach, or picnic on the lawn at ʻIolani Palace and hear the Royal Hawaiian Band play. Watch marching drills and spinning rifles at the Changing of the Guard in Waikīkī, or Okinawan taiko drumming at Kapiʻolani Park.

Honolulu Theatre for Youth
Kids are the stars at the Honolulu Theatre for Youth. Fun for the whole family. Pretend you're an octopus swimming, or dress up like a king or queen! Dive into drama, put on plays and practice screenwriting in HTY's after-school, weekend and summer programs for kids ages 5–19. Locations at Pearl City District Park and Kāneʻohe District Park. 2846 Ualena Street; www.htyweb.org • Ph: 839-9885

Hawaiʻi Theatre
Check out this cool old-fashioned theater on the edge of Chinatown. You can see circus acrobats, hula shows, music festivals, plays and film festivals here throughout the year. 1130 Bethel Street; www.hawaiitheatre.com • Ph: 528-0506

Diamond Head Theatre
See local performers star in favorite shows like *The Wizard of Oz* and *Annie* on stage at Diamond Head Theatre. Auditions for plays are held

Diamond Head Theatre offers not only fantastic shows, but classes for kids who have stars in their eyes.

throughout the year for all ages. Take classes in singing, acting, dancing and musical theatre with other kids.

Never saw a play before? Don't miss Mānoa Valley Theatre. They have great shows year-round.

Classes are for kids ages 6–13, but age limits vary for each class.
520 Makapu'u Avenue off Diamond Head Road; www.diamondhead theatre.com • Ph: 733-0274

Mānoa Valley Theatre

See comedies, new and classic plays at Mānoa Valley Theatre.
Auditions for plays are

Opera isn't just for grownups. PHOTO COURTESY OF HAWAI'I OPERA THEATRE.

held throughout the year for all ages.
2833 East Mānoa Road; www.manoavalleytheatre.com
• Ph: 988-6131

Kumu Kahua Theater

Enjoy some of the best local talent around at this 100-seat playhouse that features Hawai'i's best directors, actors and playwrights. For plays about local life, this is the venue.
46 Merchant Street; www.kumukahua.com • Ph: 536-4441

Opera is not just for adults! Join in the fun and see what it's like on and off stage.
PHOTO COURTESY OF HAWAI'I OPERA THEATRE.

Hawai'i Opera Theatre

Opera is for everyone—even kids! Sure, the younger ones might not want to sit through it, but teens will find opera is cooler than they think. Special internship programs are available for students interested in working on stage, or off stage in their wig and makeup department. Opera Previews are also available and open to all ages, and their Lānai Lectures are held an hour before any performance at which time you can learn more about what you're about to see and hear.
987 Waimanu Street; www.hawaiiopera.org • Ph: 596-7372

A scene from the production of Onegin. PHOTO COURTESY OF HAWAI'I OPERA THEATRE.

Army Community Theatre

This theatre at Fort Shafter is a fun place to see kid-friendly

Enjoy entertainment before the film at Sunset on the Beach in Waikīkī.

plays and musicals like *Alice in Wonderland* and *The Sound of Music*. Auditions for plays are held throughout the year for all ages.
Richardson Theatre at Fort Shafter; www.squareone.org/ACT • Ph: 428-4480

Leeward Community College Theatre
The best mixed-plate, local-produced plays are shown here. Kids will love the funny characters and pidgin.
96-045 Ala Ike in Pearl City • Ph: 455-0385

Sunset on the Beach Movies
See your favorite movies like *Blue Crush, Harry Potter,* and *Jurassic Park* on the big screen while cruising on the beach under the stars. A **FREE**, fun family event at Queen's Surf Beach in Waikīkī on selected weekend nights. Bring a picnic dinner or buy food from the booths. Don't miss it! Sunset on the Beach may not last forever. Visit www.co.honolulu .hi.us/

events/waikiki_events/sunset/sunset.htm for movie schedules.

Hawai'i IMAX Theatres

If you like movies, check out the Imax Theatre where the screen is five stories tall! The whole family will have fun at films like *The Lion King, Dolphins,* and *The Living Sea.*

IMAX Waikīkī at 325 Seaside Avenue • Ph: 923-4629
IMAX Polynesia at the Polynesian Cultural Center in Lāʻie • Ph: 293-3280
Check listings and showtimes at www.bigmoviezone.com.

Fun Idea!

Gather your family and friends, dress up and pretend you're going to a Hollywood movie premiere. After the film, have dinner and a post-viewing discussion—become a critic, interview your friends. See what everyone thinks.

Movie Museum

A small theater with big, cushy recliner chairs in Kaimuki. Most of the movies shown are a little weird for kids—lots of foreign films and classic oldies—but you can rent the whole place for your birthday party and show whatever movie you want!

Rent the Movie Museum Tuesdays and Wed-nesdays for $125. Bring your own food and drinks. Regular movie admission is $5.

3566 Harding Avenue, # 4 • Ph: 735-8771

Inside this unassuming store front is the Movie Museum, a Kaimukī gem—contact them to rent the space for a birthday party.

Kūhiō Beach Torch-lighting and Hula Shows

Head down to Waikīkī Beach for some **FREE** outdoor excitement. With the blowing of the conch shell and the lighting of torches, the fun begins with hula

Sign Hunt

While you're out on your adventures and excursions around O'ahu, here's a car game you can play while driving to your next activity.

Try to find these signs. Add up your points at the end. Anyone can play and any number of kids can join. Whoever sees the sign first receives the points. They could be anywhere on the island, so keep your eyes peeled! Good luck.

C. (3 points)

B. (3 points)

LEX BRODIE'S
701 QUEEN ST.

A. (3 points)

MALASADAS
PÃO-DÔCE

PALI LANES

TING YIN CHOP SUEY

D. (5 points)

E. (4 points)

dancing and Hawaiian music on the lawn at Kūhiō Beach. Bring your whole family and your beach chairs!

Free shows are from 6:30-7:30 p.m., Thursday through Sunday only. Near the Duke Kahanamoku statue on Kūhiō Beach at the intersection of Kalākaua and Kapahulu Avenues. • Ph: 843-8002

Changing of the Guard

Check out the exciting King's Guard in Waikīkī, a trick rifle drill team dressed in old-fashioned uniforms to look like King Kalākaua's palace guards. The changing of the guard ceremony is performed every night at 6 p.m. at King's Village in Waikīkī. **FREE**

131 Ka'iulani Avenue next to the Hyatt Regency Hotel in Waikīkī; www.kings-village.com • Ph: 944-6855

Kapiʻolani Park Bandstand

Head down to Waikīkī on Friday nights for **FREE** concerts at the Kapiʻolani Park Bandstand. Hang out on the lawn and have a picnic dinner or just chill out listening to the band play reggae, Hawaiian music, salsa or jazz. If you're lucky, you might catch a **FREE** show of swing dancing, Taiko drumming or hula. Free performances are from 5:30 to 6:30 p.m. on Fridays. On Monsarrat Avenue across from the Honolulu Zoo. • Ph: 843-8002

Royal Hawaiian Shopping Center

Check out **FREE** daily entertainment at the Royal Hawaiian Shopping Center—from hula shows and psychic fairs to steel drums and concerts by the Royal Hawaiian Band. Check the calendar on their website for current events.

2201 Kālakaua Avenue; www.hawaiishopper.com • Ph: 922-0588

Royal Hawaiian Band

Have a family picnic on the lawn of ʻIolani Palace and enjoy a **FREE** concert by the Royal Hawaiian Band. Free shows are Fridays at noon.

Located on the corner of King and Richards Streets in downtown Honolulu; www.iolanipalace.org • Ph: 522-0832/522-0823

Get on Stage!

Kids don't just belong in the audience, they belong on stage! You could be the next local celebrity, singing, dancing, and acting your way to stardom. The options are endless—from hula, gymnastics and tap dancing to acting in and creating your own plays! Here's a sample of programs for kids on O'ahu, but there are tons more. For programs in your neighborhood, look in the Yellow Pages under "Dancing Instruction," "Drama Instruction," and "Gymnastics."

Enjoy the Royal Hawaiian Band—there's no excuse, it's free! Not just for tourists, you know.

Pacific School of the Performing Arts

Have a "Summer Arts Experience" with other kids (ages 7–17) and explore music, drama and dance five days a week! Other programs for kids from birth to age 12 teach kids about creative movement, musical theater and singing.

www.pacarts.org • Ph: 394-6547

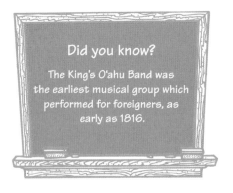
Hawai'i Academy of Performing Arts

Kids can take classes in acting, dance, piano and musical theater year-round at the Hawai'i Academy of Performing Arts.

744 South Beretania Street; www.hapa2.com • Ph: 533-3015

The Movement Center

Kids ages 2 and up can learn to sing, play instruments, tap dance, tumble, and dance hula, jazz, hip hop, ballet and more. Mommy and Me classes are fun for little ones and moms together. In Art Exploration workshops kids 5–15 can get crafty making sets and props for the annual summer performance. During holiday breaks from school, you can sign up for theater camps where you'll sing, dance, and act your way into the spotlight!

1215 Center Street #211 in Kaimukī • Ph: 735-8641

Act One

A musical theater group for kids in Kailua with classes in acting, singing and dancing. After-school, Saturday and summer (five days a week) programs for kids ages 5 –12.

411B Oneawa Street • Ph: 261-0457

'Ukulele and Hula Lessons

FREE lessons in ukulele, hula dancing, lei-making and Hawaiian quilting are offered daily at the Royal Hawaiian Shopping Center in Waikīkī.

Kids perform with gusto as part of The Movement Center. PHOTO BY CARL HEFNER, COURTESY OF THE MOVEMENT CENTER

2201 Kalākaua Avenue; www.hawaii shopper.com • Ph: 922-0588

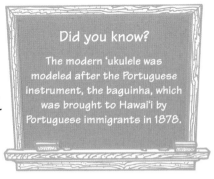

Did you know?

The modern 'ukulele was modeled after the Portuguese instrument, the baguinha, which was brought to Hawai'i by Portuguese immigrants in 1878.

7th Fret Guitar Studios

7th Fret specializes in teaching kids ages 5–12 how to play the guitar with their unique Keiki Guitar School curriculum. Youngsters learn the foundations of music, such as note reading, improvisation, solo and ensemble playing through the guitar. Young students use child-sized guitars for small hands. 7th Fret also has a curriculum for teens.
www.7thfret.com • Ph: 988-7074

Taiko Drumming Lessons

Kids ages 5 and up can take taiko drumming classes with Kenny Endo and the instructors of the Taiko Center of the Pacific at Kapi'olani Community College. Beginning, Intermediate, and Advanced levels are offered where basic form, technique, practic pieces, and cultural customs are taught.
4303 Diamond Head Road; www.kcc.hawaii.edu • Ph: 734-9448

Students of 7th Fret Guitar Studios perform at a benefit concert for Honolulu Theatre for Youth. PHOTO COURTESY OF 7TH FRET GUITAR STUDIOS.

GREAT NEIGHBORHOOD GRINDS

There are definitely plenty of 'ono grinds to find on O'ahu, and lots of fun restaurants with special kids' menus and activities. You can find just about anything—dim sum, sushi, Korean barbecue, laulau and poi, fried rice and spaghetti. Yum! When you're out on your adventure, stop for a plate lunch, some shave ice or malasadas, or snack on sushi on the beach. Here's just a small sampling of what's out there on O'ahu.

Shorts and Slippers

Big City Diner
Fun family restaurant with a large menu—great for breakfast. Huge fried rice plates, burgers, salads, milkshakes and yummy desserts. Locations in Kaimukī and Kailua—Kailua has an outside lanai.

3569 Wai'alae Avenue in Kaimuki • Ph: 738-8855
108 Hekili Street in Kailua • Ph: 263-8880

Kaka'ako Kitchen
Gourmet plate lunches, sandwiches and salads in a casual setting with an outdoor patio.

1200 Ala Moana Boulevard (at

Plate Lunch

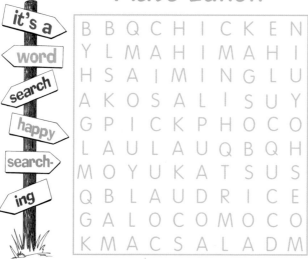

it's a word search happy search-ing

B	B	Q	C	H	I	C	K	E	N
Y	L	M	A	H	I	M	A	H	I
H	S	A	I	M	I	N	G	L	U
A	K	O	S	A	L	I	S	U	Y
G	P	I	C	K	P	H	O	C	O
L	A	U	L	A	U	Q	B	Q	H
M	O	Y	U	K	A	T	S	U	S
Q	B	L	A	U	D	R	I	C	E
G	A	L	O	C	O	M	O	C	O
K	M	A	C	S	A	L	A	D	M

Try to find all these food items and make yourself an 'ono plate lunch.
Some are horizontal, vertical, diagonal, and backwards.
Circle the ones you find.

rice	bbq chicken
poi	shoyu
kālua pig	saimin
laulau	loco moco
mac salad	katsu
mahimahi	

the end of Ward Center) • Ph: 596-7488

Dixie Grill
A fun barbecue spot with a sandbox on the patio, video games and kids eat **FREE** on special days.
404 Ward Avenue in Honolulu • Ph: 596-8359

99-016 Kamehameha Highway in ʻAiea • Ph: 485-2722

ʻOno Hawaiian Foods

Popular Hawaiian restaurant with all the favorites: lau lau, kālua pig, pipi kaula, poi, and more.

726 Kapahulu Avenue • Ph: 737-2275

Yama's Fish Market

ʻOno-licious Hawaiian plate lunches to go. Laulau, kālua pig, long rice—the works!

2332 Young Street in Moʻiliʻili • Ph: 941-9994

I Love Country Cafe

Casual hangout with a large menu of local favorites, homestyle dishes, and healthy vegetarian options.

451 Piʻikoi Street; www.ilovecountrycafe.com • Ph: 596-8108
95-1249 Meheula Parkway •
Ph: 625-5555

Kua ʻAina Sandwich Shop

Grilled burgers, kiddie burgers, mahi and tuna sandwiches are perfect with a big lemonade on a sunny day.

66-214 Kamehmeha Highway in Haleʻiwa • Ph: 637-6067
1116 Auahi Bay in Kakaʻako • Ph: 591-9133

The Chowder House

Casual seafood restaurant at Ward Warehouse.

In Ward Warehouse at 1050 Ala Moana Boulevard • Ph: 596-7944

Olive Tree Cafe

Casual Greek place next to Waiʻalae Bowl—sit outside and share pupu plates of hummus and pita bread or order a complete meal with fish, lamb, or chicken and salad.

4614 Kīlauea Avenue in Kāhala • Ph: 737-0303

Hungry Lion Coffee Shop

Lions roar and elephants trumpet in the background while you eat your fried rice or saimin. This old-time favorite local diner has a tree growing up through the middle of it and is open 24-hours a day.
1613 Nuʻuanu Avenue • Ph: 536-1188

KC Drive In

A favorite local drive-in since the 1930s with burgers, saimin and plate lunches. Try the waffle dogs for something new and different.
1029 Kapahulu Avenue • Ph: 737-5581

Boots and Kimo's Homestyle Kitchen

Laid-back diner in Kailua where the macadamia nut pancakes are yummy!
119 Hekili Street • Ph: 263-7929

The Food Company

Easy local food in Kailua—breakfast menu, plate lunches, and homestyle favorites. Hawaiian plates on Fridays only. Eat in or take it to go.
Enchanted Lake Shopping Center at 1020 Keolu Drive • Ph: 262-6440

Giovanni's Shrimp Truck

This shrimp wagon is a fun place to stop for lunch on a drive around the North Shore. Sit at the outdoor tables under the tarp and pick from tons of shrimp dishes.
Located on Kamehameha Highway in Kahuku near the Kahuku Sugar Mill • Ph: 293-1839

Zippy's

A fast favorite for local food: chili and rice, chicken katsu and

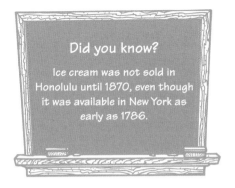
saimin. Sit down or to-go at twenty-one locations around O'ahu.

www.zippys.com • Ph: 677-8842

Matsumoto's Shave Ice
Famous for their 'ono shave ice, a great place to stop after the beach on the North Shore.

66-087 Kamehameha Highway in Hale'iwa • Ph: 637-4827

Crack Seed Store
Possibly the BEST crack seed on the island. They knew about mixing li hing sauce with mochi crunch long before it became trendy.

1156 Koko Head Avenue • Ph: 737-1022

Ronnie's Ice Cream Parlor and Restaurant
Breakfast, lunch and dinner are full of fun at Ronnie's, where guests can hoot, bark and howl when the bell clangs every time a dish comes out

There's always a line outside Matsumoto's Shave Ice.

Ono Grinds

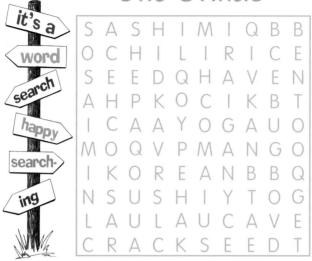

it's a word search happy search-ing

```
S A S H I M I Q B B
O C H I L I R I C E
S E E D Q H A V E N
A H P K O C I K B T
I C A A Y O G A U O
M O Q V P M A N G O
I K O R E A N B B Q
N S U S H I Y T O G
L A U L A U C A V E
C R A C K S E E D T
```

Try to find all these great grinds. Some are horizontal, vertical, diagonal, and backwards. Circle the ones you find.

shave ice	mochi
korean bbq	bento
saimin	crack seed
chili rice	laulau
sushi	mango
sashimi	papaya

from the kitchen. Big portions of local food and HUGE ice cream sundaes. A great place for birthdays. Breakfast, lunch and dinner.
98-150 Kaonohi Street in ʻAiea • Ph: 485-0995

Bubbies Homemade Ice Cream and Desserts
A huge menu of yummy desserts and homemade ice cream to choose from. Three locations around the island.
Koko Marina Shopping Center • Ph: 396-8722
Mililani Town Center • Ph: 623-5959
1010 University Avenue in Moʻiliʻili • Ph: 949-8984

All the kids in Kaimukī know about this crack seed store. It's the number one place to go after school.

Dave's Hawaiian Ice Cream Parlors
Unique local ice cream flavors like mango, lychee and kūlolo make Dave's ice cream a special treat. Chocolate-covered bananas, strawberries and cherries are also fun for kids.

Aiea: 98-820 Moanalua Road • Ph: 487-7887
Aikahi: 25 Kaneoha Bay Drive • Ph: 254-6681
Waipahu, Daiei • 94-144 Farrington Highway • Ph: 678-0355
Kāneʻohe MCBH: 1090 Selden Street • Ph: 254-3419
Kapahulu: 611 Kapahulu Avenue •

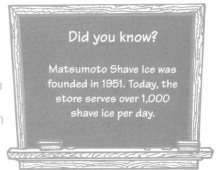

Did you know?

Matsumoto Shave Ice was founded in 1951. Today, the store serves over 1,000 shave ice per day.

Ph: 735-2194
Pearl City: 850 Kamehameha Highway • Ph: 456-8888
Sears at Ala Moana Shopping Center • Ph: 944-9663
Wai'anae: 85-786 Farrington Highway • Ph: 696-9294
Waikīkī International Market Place: 2330 Kalākaua Avenue • Ph: 926-6104
Waimānalo: 41-1537 Kalaniana'ole Highway • Ph: 259-0356
Waipi'o: 94-1040 Waipi'o Uka Street • Ph: 677-0028

Nice & Casual

Sam Choy's Breakfast, Lunch and Crab
On Tuesday nights from 5–8 p.m. a clown makes free balloon animals and there's a mini-carnival for kids in a side room. Kids can play while parents eat!
580 Nimitz Highway near K-Mart • Ph: 545-7979

Sam Choy's Diamond Head Restaurant
Gourmet restaurant with local-style dishes. A clown makes free balloon animals for kids at Sunday brunch, 10–11 a.m.
449 Kapahulu Avenue #201 • Ph: 732-8645

Irifune
Cozy Japanese spot on Kapahulu with sushi, tempura and other local dishes. Fun, but noisy and crowded on weekend nights.
563 Kapahulu Avenue • Ph: 737-1141

Little Village Noodle House
Little birds sing to you as you munch won-ton in this bamboo-covered restaurant. Casual and inexpensive.
1113 Smith Street in Chinatown • Ph: 545-3008

Wo Fat Restaurant
It looks like a Buddhist temple, but inside this historic Chinatown building the dim sum is delicious and cheap!

115 North Hotel Street • Ph: 521-5055

Old Spaghetti Factory
A kama'aina favorite for Italian food at Ward Warehouse. Check out the old trolley!
1050 Ala Moana Boulevard • Ph: 591-2513

California Pizza Kitchen
Gourmet pizza restaurant with a kid's menu.
Ala Moana Shopping Center • Ph: 941-7715
Kāhala Mall • Ph: 737-9446
Pearlridge • Ph: 487-7741

Oceanarium
A gigantic aquarium is surrounded by three restaurants at the Pacific Beach Hotel in Waikīkī. Watch eagle rays and parrotfish swim by while you dine.
Fish feeding times are exciting at noon, 1 p.m., 6:30 p.m. and 8:15 p.m.
2490 Kalākaua Avenue • Ph: 922-1233

Auntie Pasto's
Cozy Italian restaurant in Honolulu.
1099 South Beretania Street • Ph: 523-8855

Just for laughs

What do spiders eat at fast food restaurants?

Burgers and flies.

SUMMER FUN:
MORE THINGS TO DO

Still looking for something to do? How about laser tag in a giant maze? Try mini golf. Maybe some indoor rock climbing? Just open your eyes and look around—you won't know what you like until you give it a try.

Bay View Mini-Golf Park
Mini golf can be a fun adventure for the whole family! Golf around waterfalls, a banyan tree and grass huts in this tropical theme golf park. $8 for one round, $12 for two rounds. All ages.
45-285 Kāne'ohe Bay Drive • Ph: 247-0451

Jungle River Mini Golf
With a tropical rain forest theme, the outdoor 18-hole, adventure-style golf course includes a jungle village with fog, caged chameleons, a fountain bridge, and a tar pit with animal bones. There is also a video arcade and rides for keiki. $6.50 for adults, $6.00 for childen 3–10 years old and senior citizens.
98-1101 Moanalua Road, next to Pearlridge Shopping Center, Toys R Us side • Ph: 488-8808

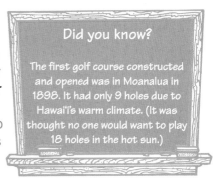

Did you know?

The first golf course constructed and opened was in Moanalua in 1898. It had only 9 holes due to Hawai'i's warm climate. (It was thought no one would want to play 18 holes in the hot sun.)

Ultrazone: The Ultimate Laser-Tag Adventure

Capture "enemy" bases and defend yourself and your base from attack with high-tech lasers at this 4,000-square-foot laser-tag arena. This futuristic experience is mind-boggling, with flashing lights and music blaring as you make your way through the foggy darkness. Ages 5 and up, $10 per person per game. Open 10 a.m. to 8 p.m. everyday, hours extended to midnight on Friday and Saturday. Located in the 'Ilikai Hotel in Waikīkī.

1777 Ala Moana Boulevard • Ph: 973-9936

Indoor Rock Climbing

Test your rock-climbing skills on the indoor wall at What's Up Gymnastics in Waipi'o. $7 for one-day pass for kids ages 5 and up and adults, groups of five or more lowers the price to $5 each.

94-485 Uke'e Street • Ph: 680-0777

Visit the Humane Society

Give some love to cats, dogs, rabbits, guinea pigs, and turtles that don't have homes at the Hawaiian Humane Society. Sign up to be a Pet Pal, or take your own dog on a Paws on the Path dog-lover's group hike. Open everyday (including holidays). **FREE**

2700 Wai'alae Avenue; www.hawaiianhumane.org • Ph: 946-2187

Polo Games

Take Mom and Dad to an exciting polo game and watch the horses thunder by as jockeys swing at the ball. Kids can visit the ponies after the game. There are two polo fields on O'ahu that have Sunday games open to the public during the polo season (March through August). Call for game times and admission charges, often **FREE** for kids under 12; $3–$5 for adults. Games usually start around 2 p.m. on Sundays.

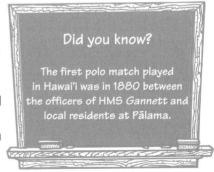

Did you know?

The first polo match played in Hawai'i was in 1880 between the officers of HMS *Gannett* and local residents at Pālama.

Waimānalo Polo Field: 41-741 Kalaniana'ole Highway • Ph: 396-0494 Mokulē'ia Polo Field: 411 Farrington Highway • Ph: 949-0061

Bargain shopping at its best—only at the Aloha Stadium Swap Meet.

Swap Meet
Search for bargains at the Aloha Stadium Swap Meet, like one massive garage sale and craft fair put together. Open 8 a.m. to 4 p.m. on Wednesday, Saturday and Sunday. Admission is $0.50 per person. Located in the parking lot surrounding Aloha Stadium at 99-500 Salt Lake Boulevard. • Ph: 486-6704

Join a Sports Team!
Playing on a soccer, baseball, or softball team is a great way to make friends and have fun in the sun. Contact the following organizations to find out what teams are practicing in your neighborhood:
Hawai'i Youth Soccer Association (HYSA)
www.hawaiisoccer.com
951-4972

DA KINE PIDGIN 2

ACROSS

2. Steal.
3. Eat.
5. Don't talk badly about someone.
6. Dirty look.
8. Chat, share stories, gossip.

DOWN

1. Stink!
2. Plenty.
3. Guaranteed
4. No good.
5. Don't be shy or embarrassed.
7. Take it easy.
9. Please. (——— come!)

Fun Idea!
Gather your friends and start your own book club. You can meet at the library to have discussions then head to the nearest shave ice place for some sweet fun.

American Youth Soccer Organization (AYSO)
www.soccer.org
696-8889

Little League Baseball
www.littleleague.org
262-2405

Hawai'i Amateur Softball Association
www.hawaiiasa.com
523-4757

Fun Idea!
Still need some ideas of what to do that you haven't yet done? Volunteer! You can make a difference by helping others.

Learn Martial Arts
O'ahu has hundreds of dojos that offer classes for kids in karate, jiu-jitsu, tae kwon do, capeoira (a Brazilian martial art), kick-boxing, and more. To find a dojo near you, look up "Martial Arts Instruction" in the Yellow Pages, or visit www.onzuka.com/oahu.html.

Check out the Library!
Libraries are more fun than you might think. Hang out in the kids' section and discover a new book. Most libraries have special keiki storytelling hours; call the library nearest you to find out when. All libraries are closed on Sundays.

'Aiea Public Library
99-143 Moanalua Road; 483-7333

'Āina Haina Public Library
5246 Kalaniana'ole Highway; 377-2456

'Ewa Beach Public and School Library
91-950 North Road; 689-1204

Hawai'i Kai Public Library
249 Lunalilo Home Road; 397-5833

Hawai'i State Library
478 South King Street; 586-3500

Kahuku Public and School Library
56-490 Kamehameha Highway; 293-8935

Kailua Public Library
239 Ku'ulei Road; 266-9911
Kaimukī Public Library
1041 Koko Head Avenue; 733-8422

Kalihi-Pālama Public Library
1325 Kalihi Street; 832-3466

Kāneʻohe Public Library
45-829 Kamehameha Highway;
233-5676

Kapolei Public Library
1020 Manawai Street

Library for the Blind and
Physically Handicapped
402 Kapahulu Avenue; 733-8444

Liliha Public Library
1515 Liliha Street; 587-7577

Mānoa Public Library
2716 Woodlawn Drive; 988-0459

McCully-Mōʻiliʻili Public Library
2211 South King Street;
973-1099

Mililani Public Library
95-450 Makaimoimo Street;
627-7470

Pearl City Public Library
1138 Waimano Home Road;
453-6566

Salt Lake/Moanalua Public
Library
3225 Salt Lake Boulevard;
831-6831

Wahiawā Public Library
820 California Avenue; 622-6345

Waialua Public Library
67-068 Kealohanui Street; 637-8286

Waiʻanae Public Library
85-625 Farrington Highway; 697-7868

Waikīkī-Kapahulu Public
Library
400 Kapahulu Avenue;
733-8488

Waimānalo Public and
School Library
41-1320 Kalanianaole
Highway; 259-2610

Waipahu Public Library
94-275 Mokuola Street;
675-0358

The Hawaiʻi State Library—check it out!

Oh, the Places You'll Go

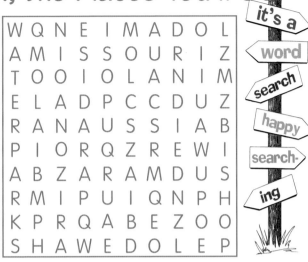

```
W Q N E I M A D O L
A M I S S O U R I Z
T O O I O L A N I M
E L A D P C C D U Z
R A N A U S S I A B
P I O R Q Z R E W I
A B Z A R A M D U S
R M I P U I Q N P H
K P R Q A B E Z O O
S H A W E D O L E P
```

Try to find all these great places to visit. Some are horizontal, vertical, diagonal, and backwards. Circle the ones you find.

aquarium	Paradise
zoo	Waimea
Bishop	Dole
Arizona	Damien
waterpark	PCC
'Iolani	

Volunteer!

Interested in working with younger kids? Want to help protect the environment? Volunteerhawaii.org, a website launched by United Way, provides a listing of over 100 volunteer opportunities for kids—from helping with the Special Olympics, to learning more about marine life.

www.volunteerhawaii.org

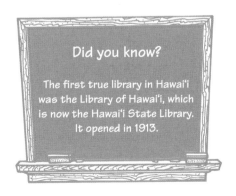

Did you know?

The first true library in Hawai'i was the Library of Hawai'i, which is now the Hawai'i State Library. It opened in 1913.

SPECIAL EVENTS

Check your calendar. What month is it? There might be something exciting going on around town. Maybe a kite-flying contest or craft fair. A carnival or parade. You never know what you might be missing.

JANUARY

Whale Watching
Cruise down to the South Shore from Waikīkī to Makapuʻu between December and April to look for humpback whales off the coast.

Ala Wai Challenge
Watch a competition of Hawaiian sports and games, ending with an exciting canoe race. Waikīkī • Ph: 923-1802

Narcissus Festival
Before Chinese New Year, this festival includes a queen pageant, cooking demonstrations, a fashion show and cultural fair. Honolulu • Ph: 533-3181

Chinese New Year's Celebration
Check out the lion dances, fireworks displays, and food booths in Chinatown for this annual event.
Late January or early February.
Chinatown • Ph: 533-3181

Take your parents on a picnic and drive up to the North Shore to watch the professionals body surf. PHOTO © DOUGLAS PEEBLES.

Pipeline Bodysurfing Classic
A top world-class bodysurfing competition held at North Shore's Banzai Pipeline. 'Ehukai Beach Park • Ph: 638-8825

FEBRUARY

Punahou Carnival
A huge carnival in early February at Punahou School in Mānoa. Rides, games, a thrift market and tons of food booths. Honolulu • Ph: 944-5711

NFL Pro Bowl
Check out the best players in pro football at the last game of the season at Aloha Stadium • Ph: 233-4NFL

Hawai'i Marine Artist Youth Competition
Sea Life Park hosts this annual art competition and display. Waimānalo • Ph: 259-7933

Vroom, vroom! Ride in style at the Punahou carnival.

MARCH

Hawai'i Polo Club Games
Games are every Sunday throughout the spring and summer, from early March through August. Waimānalo and Mokulē'ia • Ph: 637-7656

Oahu Kite Festival
This exciting festival has kite demonstrations, kite ballet, kite battles and some of the world's largest kites. Kapi'olani Park • Ph: 735-9059

Cherry Blossom Festival
This annual Japanese heritage celebration runs from January through March, with many public events like parades, heritage fairs and taiko drumming festivals • Ph: 949-2255

The Great Hawaiian Rubber Duckie Race
Watch more than 20,000 rubber ducks race down the Ala Wai Canal for charity. Donate money to race your own rubber ducky! Waikīkī • Ph: 532-6744

Taiko Drumming Festival
See and hear taiko drummers from Los Angeles, Japan and Hawai'i at the Blaisdell Center • Ph: 591-2211

APRIL

Buddha Day
Pageants, dances and flower celebrations at Buddhist temples all around the island on the closest Sunday to April 8 • Ph: 536-7044

Hawaiian Scottish Festival & Games
Scottish games, competitions, food, dancing, and pipe bands at Kapi'olani Park • Ph: 235-7605

MAY

May Day is Lei Day Celebration
May 1 celebration with flowers, a lei-making contest, and a May Day Queen coronation at Kapi'olani Park • Ph: 547-7393

Hawai'i State Fair
This fair with rides, music, food and crafts at Aloha Stadium starts on Memorial Day weekend and runs for one month • Ph: 486-9300

JUNE

King Kamehameha Celebration Floral Parade
Kamehameha's birthday, June 11, is a state holiday and there is a major parade with floral floats and colorful pa'u riders on horseback that runs from downtown Honolulu to Waikīkī • Ph: 586-0333

King Kamehameha Hula Competition
This hula competition at the Blaisdell draws dancers from around the world. Honolulu • Ph: 536-6540

Pacific Island Taro Festival
A two-day festival at Windward Community College that celebrates the cultures and traditions of the Pacific Islands with music, storytelling, dancing, and every kind of taro dish imaginable. Kāne'ohe • Ph: 235-7433

Hawaiian Professional Rodeo
Watch expert rodeo riders and bullfighting while enjoying the outdoor barbecue, live country music and dancing. Also in August. Waimānalo • Ph: 259-9941

JULY

Fourth of July Macfarland Canoe Regatta at Waikīkī Beach
The most exciting event of the summer paddling season when outrigger canoe teams catch waves and race towards the beach. Waikīkī.

Fourth of July Parade & Fireworks
Celebrate the Fourth with a parade through Kailua town and fireworks at Kailua Beach Park. Kailua • Ph: 263-2076

A Midsummer Night's Gleam
A free enchanted evening at Foster Botanical Garden when the entire garden is lit with paper lanterns. Butterfly princesses and belly dancers,

Don't miss Fourth of July fireworks lighting the beaches of Waikīkī. PHOTO © DOUGLAS PEEBLES.

and musicians with harps and bagpipes wander through the garden. Fortune telling, giant bubble-blowing and other activities are fun for kids. Downtown • Ph: 522-7060/537-1708

The "Wildest Show in Town"
A free evening concert at the Honolulu Zoo on Wednesday evenings from mid-July through August. • Ph: 926-3191

Bankoh Na Wahine O Hawai'i
Hawai'i's best women Hawaiian singers and dancers perform at this free festival at Ala Moana Beach Park. • Ph: 522-7030

Hawai'i State Farm Fair
A real country fair with entertainment, farm animals and a petting zoo, food booths and rides. • Ph: 848-2074

Hawai'i International Jazz Festival
Four days of jazz concerts in Honolulu. • Ph: 528-0506

'Ukulele Festival
Performances by Hawai'i's best 'ukulele performers and a 250-piece keiki 'ukulele band. Honolulu • Ph: 732-3739

Queen Lili'uokalani Keiki Hula Competition
Prestigious hula competition for keiki dancers at Blaisdell Center. Late July or early August. • Ph: 521-6905

AUGUST

Floating Lantern Ceremony
A Buddhist ceremony in which floating lanterns are sailed on small boats to light the way to eternal rest for the spirits of ancestors. Ala Wai Field and Park. • Ph: 595-2556

Hawai'i Dragon Boat Festival
Teams from around the world race in colorful Dragon Boats at Ala Moana Beach Park. • Ph: 951-0350

Hawaiian Slack Key Festival

Slack-key guitar musicians perform at the McCoy Pavilion in Ala Moana Park. • Ph: 592-2288

Greek Festival

A celebration of Greek food, music and culture at the McCoy Pavilion in Ala Moana Beach Park. • Ph: 521-7220

Aloha Festivals Week is a great time to enjoy music, dancing, food and parades. Photo © Douglas Peebles.

SEPTEMBER

Plantation Heritage Festival

A celebration of the plantation days at Waipahu Cultural Garden Park. Waipahu • Ph: 677-0110

Downtown Hoʻolauleʻa

A massive free block party in downtown Honolulu marks the beginning of the Aloha Festivals with food booths and entertainment. • Ph: 545-1771

Aloha Festivals

Hawaiian music festivals, concerts and parades from early September to mid-October. • Ph: 589-1771

Okinawan Festival

Cultural festival at Kapiʻolani Park with dancing and food. • Ph: 676-5400

A stately paʻū rider in the Aloha Festivals parade. Photo © Douglas Peebles.

Pick your own pumpkin to carve at the Kapolei Pumpkin Patch.

OCTOBER

Talk Story Festival
Hawai'i's top storytellers tell legends at the McCoy Pavilion in Ala Moana Park. • Ph: 973-7262

Vans G-Shock Triple Crown of Surfing Series
Men's and women's professional world-class big-wave surfing competitions on the North Shore. Late October to December. • Ph: 337-2323

Waimea Falls Makahiki Festival
Hawaiian cultural festival at Waimea Falls Adventure Park with Hawaiian games, crafts, music, food and a major hula competition. • Ph: 638-8511

Great Kapolei Pumpkin Patch
Pick up your own Halloween pumpkins at Aloun Farms in 'Ewa. Hay rides, petting zoos, ponies and more. Located on Farrington Highway between Waipahu and Kapolei at 91-1440 Farrington Highway. • Ph: 677-9516, ext. 43

NOVEMBER

E Hoi Mai i ka Piko Hula: The World Invitational Hula Festival
The best hula dancers from around the world gather for ancient and modern hula competitions. • Ph: 486-3185

DECEMBER

Candlelight Christmas at Mission Houses Museum
A living history Christmas celebration with actors in early 19th-century costumes, caroling, and storytelling. Honolulu • Ph: 531-0481

Honolulu City Lights

A Christmas tree-lighting ceremony with a 50-foot tree followed by a concert at Honolulu Hale, then all of downtown is lit with thousands of lights. Either drive through downtown, walk or take a carriage ride. Train rides for kids. • Ph: 527-5784

Honolulu Marathon

Cheer on the thousands of runners who take over the streets from Waikīkī to Hawai'i Kai and back, ending at the Kapi'olani Park Bandstand. • Ph: 734-7200

Christmas Craft Fairs

Check the newspaper for the dates, times and locations of the many craft fairs held at Christmas time.

Honolulu's Christmas lights turn all of downtown into a winter wonderland—minus the snow.
Photo © Douglas Peebles.

LET'S PLAN A DAY

Take a trip in your own backyard! You don't have to get on an airplane to find new adventures. Pack up the kids and the car and go for a road trip around the island. How often do you get out to the wild and wonderful North Shore? Cruise the country not far from home in Waimānalo. Explore the mystery and magic of old Honolulu and Chinatown. Break out of your boring routine and get back in touch with the things you really love about Hawai'i.

Day Trip 1: Circle Island Drive to the North Shore

Where: Drive up the east coast along Kamehameha Highway (to get there from Town, take the Pali Highway or H-3 until you meet up with Kamehameha Highway heading north) all the way to the North Shore, then back to Town on H-2 and H-1.

When to Go: During the summer (May through August) you'll encounter sunny beaches and calm water. During the winter (October through April) swimming is out of the question because of the dangerous ocean conditions, but the huge waves and surfing competitions are exciting to

Chinaman's Hat, known as Mokoliʻi, is said to be a giant lizard's tail. The moʻo Mokoliʻi fought and was destroyed by the goddess Hiʻiaka. When it fell, its tail became this islet, and its body the flat land near the old sugar mill in Kāneʻohe. Photo © Douglas Peebles

watch. Leave early in the morning (around 8 or 9) for a fun-filled day of new adventures.

What to Bring: Swimsuits, sunscreen (SPF 15 or higher), bottled water, mask and snorkel, shoes or slippers, towels, and snacks or a picnic lunch.

Get out of town and take a family trip to the North Shore! During the summertime (May through August) the ocean is calm, the sand is warm and the skies are crystal clear for miles. Head out right after breakfast and drive the long way up Kamehameha Highway on the east side for some out-of-the-ordinary sights.

One of the first sights along Kamehameha Highway after Kāneʻohe is **Mokoliʻi Island**, also known as **Chinaman's**

Hat. The Hawaiians believed the small cone shaped island you see off of Kualoa Regional Park was the tail of a giant lizard dragon killed by the volcano goddess Pele's younger sister, Hi'iaka. Mokoli'i means "small lizard" in Hawaiian. The island was later named Chinaman's Hat by islanders who thought it resembled the cone-shaped hat worn by Chinese plantation workers.

On the mauka side of the road is **Kualoa Ranch**, the largest working cattle ranch on Oahu. Parts of the movie "Jurassic Park" were filmed here.

Down the road, after the town of Ka'a'awa, you'll come to **Crouching Lion Inn**, a restaurant and inn built in 1927. The inn is named for the large rock on the ridge above it that some say looks like a lion lying on his belly. Around the bend is **Kahana Bay**. On the makai side of the road you'll

Have a sandcastle building contest at Mālaekahana Beach Park. Photo © Douglas Peebles

see **Huilua Fishpond**, built by the Hawaiians more than four hundred years ago.

If you're ready for brunch or lunch at this point, stop at **Punalu'u Restaurant** (formerly Ahi's, at 53-146 Kamehameha Hwy) for a mountain of fresh shrimp or a burger. Back in the car, drive through **Hau'ula**, then pass the **Polynesian Cultural Center** on the left in the town of **Lā'ie**. After the **Lā'ie Shopping Center**, follow the signs to the incredible **Mormon Temple** at the end of Hale La'a Blvd. just off the highway on the left-hand side.

Heading back up Kamehameha Highway, you'll come to **Mālaekahana State Recreation Area**. If you're looking for a place to stop and swim, this is your first promising opportunity, but it won't be your last. Pull in at the first yellow sign and park in the dirt parking lot. Don't leave any valuables in the car. Walk up on the paved pathway just past the four handicapped parking stalls. A white arrow that reads "Picnic Area" will guide you. Walk out to **Kalanai Point** for a picnic on a grassy field surrounded by shady ironwood trees. There are restrooms, showers and picnic tables. The beach here is good for swimming and snorkeling, and if the tide is low, you can wade out to **Moku'auia Island** (also known as "Goat Island"). There is no lifeguard here, so parents, please watch children in the water.

Heading north again, you'll pass the **Kahuku Shrimp Farm** on your right. In these manmade pools, delicious shrimp are raised and then sold to restaurants all around the island. In the town of Kahuku, the **Kahuku Sugar Mill** is a fading reminder of Hawai'i's sugar plantation era. Visitors can take a self-guided tour between 9 a.m. and 5 p.m. to see the huge machinery used to crush sugarcane and turn it into raw brown sugar.

After the **Turtle Bay Resort**, you'll come to **Sunset Beach**. The beaches of **Sunset**, **'Ehukai**, and **Banzai** are stacked one after another here, but for the best summertime swimming, keep your pants on for what's coming up around the bend. At **Pūpūkea**, take a left immediately after the **Foodland** (a good place to stop for water, snacks, and any forgotten supplies) on Pupukea Road. Follow the signs to the **Pu'u o Mahuka Heiau**, the remains of an ancient Hawaiian temple with incredible views of Waimea Bay from above. This is the largest surviving Hawaiian temple on O'ahu-it covers about 5 acres. Please do not touch the lava rocks or offerings. Take a stroll around the lava rock heiau, then head back down the hill to Kamehameha Highway and go left towards **Waimea Bay**.

Sit and watch surfers rip the curling waves, or simply take in the outstanding view at Waimea Bay. Photo © Douglas Peebles

Waimea Bay is known for its massive (and dangerous) waves during the winter surf season, but during the summertime it is usually glassy and calm like a pond. Park in the lot (don't leave any valuables), and head down to the beach. There are picnic tables, showers and restrooms near the parking lot. Walk down to the Pūpūkea end of the beach to snorkel among huge underwater boulders. Kids can skimboard and bodysurf. Beware of the large rock on the west end of the beach—older kids and adults jump off this rock into the crashing waves below, but it is not recommended.

After sunning, swimming and snorkeling at Waimea, keep going up Kamehameha Highway and take the turnoff to the town of **Hale'iwa**. Here you'll find shops, restaurants and crafts, another great place to stop for a bite to eat. Don't miss **Matsumoto Shave Ice** for the best shave ice on the island, no joke! Try **Kua 'Aina** for big juicy burgers and mahi sandwiches. Continue on down the road to the **North Shore Marketplace** where you'll find the **North Shore Surf and Cultural Museum**, a free surfing museum with antique surfboards and surf videos playing all day long.

From Hale'iwa you can follow Kamehameha Highway to H-2 to head back to Honolulu (if that's where you're coming from). If you're still up for an adventure, make a quick stop in Wahiawā at the **Kukaniloko Birthstones State Monument** on Whitmore Avenue, where you'll find mystical stones in a grove of trees surrounded by pineapple fields. These stones were used centuries ago by Hawaiian royalty—it was believed that giving birth on these stones would give the royal children more mana, or power. Take a look around, imagine Hawai'i's mystical past, and take a deep breath as you jump back in the car to head back home.

Day Trip 2: Cruising the South Shore to Waimānalo

Where: On O'ahu's south and southeast shores, between Hawai'i Kai and Kailua. Follow Kalaniana'ole Highway along this entire route.

When to Go: Any time of year, but head out in the morning because the Ko'olau mountains block the sun by mid-afternoon on this side of the island. Check the weather report before you go, the windward side can often be cloudy, overcast and rainy throughout the year.

What to Bring: Hiking shoes, swimsuits, towels, sunscreen (SPF 15 or higher), mosquito repellent, boogie boards or skimboards, water, meat tenderizer (in case of man-o-war stings), snacks and a picnic lunch.

Start early for a full day of adventures on the South Shore. If you're heading out from Honolulu, take Kalaniana'ole Highway past Hawai'i Kai, heading east. As you drive along the rugged lava rock cliffs you'll have spectacular views of the ocean below. You'll pass **Hanauma Bay** on your right and **Koko Crater** on your left. Stop off at the scenic lookout and watch the seaspray shoot from **Hālona**

If you have time, stop and snorkel at Hanauma Bay. Take a fish ID card with you and see who can identify the most fish. PHOTO © DOUGLAS PEEBLES

Fly kites or buy some windsocks at Sandy Beach Park. The wind really picks up and can make your kite soar.

Blowhole, then peek over the other side of the lookout to see **Cockroach Cove**, a tiny beach also known as "From Here to Eternity" Beach because the sandy love scene from the movie was filmed here.

Head further east along Kalaniana'ole Highway and you'll pass **Sandy Beach Park**, a popular beach with experienced bodyboarders, where the currents are strong and wave conditions are too dangerous for kids. After Sandys, you'll pass the Hawai'i Kai Golf Course on your left, and as you round the bend you'll start to go uphill. Halfway up the hill you'll pass an unmarked black metal gate on your right. Pull over and park on the side of the highway for a trek up the hill to the **Makapu'u Lighthouse**. Make sure you bring water with you because the trail can be hot and very dry. It's

The hike to the Makapu'u Lighthouse is fun and easy for all ages. See the hiking chapter for information. Photo © Douglas Peebles

about 3 miles round trip.

Go through or around the gate to find the rocky path-it becomes paved further on and is easy to follow. You'll hike through lava and haole koa as the trail winds up the side of the hill then wraps around the ocean side where you'll

How did Rabbit Island get its name? It's not just because this large island off Waimanalo is shaped like a rabbit's head with the ears lying flat. In the late 1800s a rancher decided to breed rabbits on the island. Today Rabbit Island is a protected seabird sanctuary, but it is rumored that a few rabbits still live there to this day.

get stunning views of the Pacific and the windward coast. Keep an eye out for **humpback whales** if it's their season in Hawai'i—from December through April—because they often spout and breech off of Makapu'u. At the top you'll end up at a lookout just above the lighthouse, where you can peer over the cliff to watch the surfers and bodyboarders down below at **Makapu'u Beach**, a hotspot for O'ahu's most experienced wave riders. Back to the car it's all downhill, no sweat.

Heading east along Kalaniana'ole Highway again you'll pass the entrance to **Makapu'u Beach Park** on your right, best left to the pros. On your left is **Sea Life Park**, a fun aquatic park for kids, with a huge aquarium, dolphin shows, sea lions and a sea turtle habitat. As you round the bend you enter **Waimānalo**, a small seaside town not far from Honolulu that still feels like country.

With **Rabbit Island** on your right, continue on until you come to **Waimānalo Beach Park**. This is a great place to stop, swim, and wash off the dust from your hike. The whole family can boogie board and swim, then have a picnic lunch. If you didn't pack a lunch, you can pick up supplies at **Mel's Market** down the road or order plate lunches at **Keneke's**. Everything in Waimānalo is within a five-minute drive.

After your lunch has settled and you've caught your last wave, continue on down the highway into Waimanalo "town." Turn left onto **Kumuhau** Street, which will take you through the backroads of the area-you'll follow the base of the majestic Koʻolau mountains as you drive past **plant and flower nurseries**, **horse stables** and **farms**. When you emerge back on the main highway, top off your day at the Waimanalo Town Center for a special **Dave's Ice Cream** treat in island flavors like lychee, kūlolo and mango.

From here, you can either turn around and go back the way you came or continue down Kalaniʻanaʻole Highway past Kailua until it meets up with the Pali Highway at Castle Hospital. To get back to Town and H-1 from here, take a left at Castle Hospital and follow the signs.

While you're in Waimanalo, grab a snack. There's shave ice, or hot malasadas you can try.

Day Trip 3: Old Honolulu and Chinatown

Where: Historic Honolulu and Chinatown are located between Nimitz Highway, River Street, Vineyard Boulevard and Bethel Street. Park in the lot next to Aloha Tower off Nimitz Highway at Pier 7 in Honolulu Harbor. This walking tour is better for older kids who don't mind walking a lot. A warning for parents: Old Chinatown can be a little funky in some spots. Don't try this tour at night.

When to Go: Anytime! Visit Chinatown during Chinese New Year (late January to early February) for extra fun and entertainment. This is great trip to take when the weather's no good for the beach.

What to Bring: Comfortable walking shoes, a stroller for little kids, hats and sunglasses, bottled water, extra spending money.

Take a trip into Hawai'i's past and rediscover the rich history of downtown Honolulu. Start out your day with a climb to the top of **Aloha Tower**, the ten-story clock tower that was the tallest

Not only can you get some exercise walking up to the top of Aloha Tower, but you can get some fun shopping in as well. Photo © Douglas Peebles

building in Hawai'i for many years (don't worry, you can take the elevator). Aloha Tower is located off Nimitz Highway on the waterfront of **Honolulu Harbor**. There's lots of parking in the nearby lots, free with validation and a $5 purchase at one of the **Aloha Tower Marketplace** shops or restaurants. From the top of the tower, you'll have a bird's-eye view of the ships in Honolulu Harbor on one side, and downtown Honolulu stretching all the way back to the Ko'olau mountains on the other. This is a great way to get oriented as you begin your downtown adventure.

The *Hōkūle'a* out at sea. Learn more about how Native Hawaiians navigated way back when. PHOTO © DOUGLAS PEEBLES

Along the harbor to the east you'll see the historic *Falls of Clyde*, built in 1878 in Scotland. The *Hōkūle'a*, Hawai'i's world-famous Polynesian voyaging canoe, is docked right behind the *Falls of Clyde*. Both ships can be toured for a fee through the **Hawai'i Maritime Center** at Pier 7. Inside of the Maritime Center is the full skeleton of a humpback whale. There's only one other in the whole world so don't miss it!

When you're ready to leave the waterfront,

walk one block towards 'Ewa (left when facing the mountains) on Nimitz and turn right on Bethel Street. At the corner of Merchant and Bethel, you'll pass some of Hawai'i's **oldest and most famous buildings**: the Kamehameha V Post Office (built in 1870), Yokohama Specie Bank (built in 1909), and the former Honolulu Police Station (built in 1931). They sure don't build 'em like these anymore!

Continue walking up Bethel Street until you pass the large fountain in the courtyard behind **Indigo Restaurant**. On the corner of Pauahi Street, you'll find the **Hawai'i Theatre**, a beautiful historic theater where you can catch concerts, plays, films and even circus acts. Ask to take a peek inside if there isn't a performance going on. Take a left down Pauahi, walk two blocks until you reach Smith Street. On your right is a small park with benches and a basketball court. Half a block down Smith Street on your left you'll find **Little Village Noodle House**, a fun place to stop for lunch. Little birds chirp in the background as you munch on potstickers or slurp noodle soup beneath the vine-covered bamboo canopy.

After you've fueled up on lunch, keep walking makai (towards the ocean) on Smith Street, and take a right on Hotel Street. Walk one block until you meet up with Maunakea Street, the heart of Honolulu's Chinatown. On the far corner you'll see **Wo Fat Chop Sui**, one of Honolulu's oldest and most famous Chinese restaurants. Half a block mauka up Maunakea Street is the **Maunakea Marketplace**, a maze of Chinese specialty shops, restaurants, and meat, fish and vegetable vendors. Head makai down Maunakea Street and you'll find sweet-smelling lei shops, antique stores, Chinese herbalists, and bakeries. Don't miss the **Shung Chong Yuein Chinese Cake Shop** at 1027 Maunakea Street where delicious candies and pastries line the glass window-moon cakes, almond cookies, peanut candy and candied papaya, pineapple, coconut and lotus make excellent snacks for tired little walkers.

Now head down Maunakea Street a half-block toward the ocean and turn left on N. King Street to check out some of Honolulu's most famous landmarks. You'll pass **Fort**

There's some great finds in Chinatown—from food to trinkets to antiques.

Street Mall, a walking-only street with shops and restaurants. Three blocks later, on the corner of Richards and King Streets, you'll reach the magnificent grounds of **'Iolani Palace**, the only official royal palace in the entire United States! It costs $5–15 to tour the official residence of Hawai'i's last monarchs, but the palace grounds are open to the public and **FREE**. Take a moment to sit in the grass beneath the palms, or check out the **Coronation Pavilion**, where the Royal Hawaiian Band plays **FREE** concerts on Fridays at noon.

Right next door to the palace is the **Hawai'i State Library**, a cool air-conditioned retreat from the hot city streets. A cool kid's reading section and outdoor courtyards make it a worthwhile place to visit.

Cross King Street from the library to reach the **Mission Houses Museum**, where you can tour some of the first wood-

Want to feel royal? Have a seat on the lawn and enjoy the Royal Hawaiian Band in front of 'Iolani Palace.

frame houses ever built in Hawai'i. Walk through the bedrooms and kitchens of the early missionary families and see how they lived almost two hundred years ago. Head back down King Street towards Chinatown and you'll come to **Kawaiaha'o Church**, a beautiful church built in 1841 of coral cut from Hawai'i's reefs. The church offers public services on Sunday mornings that are preached in Hawaiian and English, and **FREE** tours are offered Sundays after the services and weekdays (call ahead to schedule a tour). Many of the descendants of Hawai'i's early missionaries are buried in the small graveyard behind the church. Make sure to take a peek inside the church and explore the grounds.

On King Street across from the palace is **Ali'iōlani Hale**, home of the Hawai'i State Supreme Court. Out front, the famous **statue of King Kamehameha I** is often draped with beautiful lei.

To get back to Aloha Tower Marketplace parking lots, head one block toward Chinatown down King Street until you reach Richards Street. Take a left here and head toward the harbor. Richards Street will take you straight to the large parking lot at Piers 5 and 6. Aloha Tower will be further down to the right.

ANSWERS TO
WORD SEARCHES &
CROSSWORDS

ANSWERS

Life's A Beach

```
K A O W P I A K O P
E L B E L L O W S U
H A W A I K I K I N
O M N U U A C A N A
E O S H E I E L W L
N A E M S L W A K U
A N I O O U A M P U
K A W A K A H A N A
W D S A N S O U C I
S H E R W O O D S P
```

page 4

Tidepools

```
H S S T A R F I S H
I E C O R A B C H R
R A R E L L E A U O
S F A M E E D F M C
E O B A I L O I L K
A U S M I T C S F S
W S E A U R C H I N
E T C O R A L R M T
E A F A T H C M A K
D O C S H E L L S B
```

page 9

Surf's Up

page 19

Water Sports

```
C K I T E S U R F S
A B S N O R K E L A
N O W A T E R S K I
O D G I N A C U G L
E Y U R N R K R D S
V B W A T D L F E O
L O P A R A S A I L
K A Y A K F W U K S
W R D I V I N G R R
H D F G N I H S I F
```

page 25

Picnic in the Park

```
A L A M O A N A L I
K F W H N U U A N U
M O A N A L U A W A
A S H L U H L U H R
L T I K A O Y T A K
Y E A M I W O S I U
K R W P O A N F K A
U H A L E I W A U L
A K E U U T E R Y O
H O O M A L U H I A
```

page 34

Rumble in the Jungle

```
M A M A K I H E L O
A I R O N W O O D G
I A L T E L N M K L
L O O W V A T A U A
E V A K O A M O K K
R I A M A I E G U A
K O H E L O P T I N
O H A I A L E H U A
M R K A V A U G N W
T P A N I N I R O N
```

page 53

Hawaiian Language 101

page 55

What Do You Know About Hawaiʻi?

page 57

Hawaiian Language 202

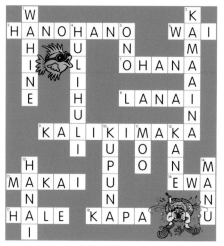

```
W                       K
H A N O H A N O     W A I
  H           N       M
  I       O H A N A   A
  I           N       A
  N         L A N A I N
  E         U         A
    K A L I K I M A K A
      I     U   O   N
    H       P   O   N   M
  M A K A I U       E W A
    N       U           N
  H A L E   K A P A     U
    I
```

page 66

Hiking

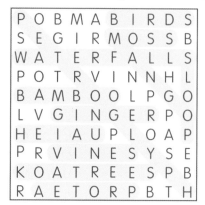

```
P O B M A B I R D S
S E G I R M O S S B
W A T E R F A L L S
P O T R V I N N H L
B A M B O O L P G O
L V G I N G E R P O
H E I A U P L O A P
P R V I N E S Y S E
K O A T R E E S P B
R A E T O R P B T H
```

page 86

Da Kine Pidgin

```
C H I C K E N S K I N
A       A         O
N       A Y       O A C
A     D E M       D A T
B       E
D A K I N E
A       U
B A M B U C H A       H
R       U       L O L O
O     M A N I N I     W
K       B       I D A Z
E       Y           Z I
        E     F U T   T
```

page 96

Wheels

```
R A Z E R I C K H N H W
W O B I C Y C L E I W I
A E L C Y C I N U N H N
G L B L C Y C L E I E I
O S A I E I N G E R E R
N K O S A R I S L E L E
T A N D E M B I K E E T
L A B I A U Q L Y O Y O
T R I C Y C L E A O S O
Q B L A U D R I C D C C
I N L I N E S K A T E S
M O U N T A I N B I K E
```

page 111

Plate Lunch

```
B B Q C H I C K E N
Y L M A H I M A H I
H S A I M I N G L U
A K O S A L I S U Y
G P I C K P H O C O
L A U L A U Q B Q H
M O Y U K A T S U S
Q B L A U D R I C E
G A L O C O M O C O
K M A C S A L A D M
```

page 126

'Ono Grinds

```
S A S H I M I Q B B
O C H I L I R I C E
S E E D Q H A V E N
A H P K O C I K B T
I C A A Y O G A U O
M O Q V P M A N G O
I K O R E A N B B Q
N S U S H I Y T O G
L A U L A U C A V E
C R A C K S E E D T
```

page 130

Da Kine Pidgin 2

page 138

Oh, the Places You'll Go

```
W Q N E I M A D O L
A M I S S O U R I Z
T O O I O L A N I M
E L A D P C C D U Z
R A N A U S S I A B
P I O R Q Z R E W I
A B Z A R A M D U S
R M I P U I Q N P H
K P R Q A B E Z O O
S H A W E D O L E P
```

page 141

BIBLIOGRAPHY

Applebaum, Julie. *Fun With the Family in Hawaii*. Guilford, Conn: Globe Pequot Press, 2001.

Ball, Stuart M. Jr. *The Hikers Guide to Oʻahu*. Honolulu: University of Hawaiʻi Press, 2000.

Cook, Terri. *Family Guide to Honolulu and the Island of Oahu*. Honolulu: Hawaiian Service, Inc., 1977.

Clark, John R. K. *The Beaches of Oahu*. Honolulu: University of Hawaiʻi Press, 1977.

Davidson, Dana, et al. *Hawaii For Kids: A Family Guide to the Islands*. Honolulu: Bess Press, 1990.

Drake, Jane, and Ann Love. *The Kids' Summer Handbook*. New York: Ticknor & Fields, 1994.

Fun and Games: Small Kid Time in Hawaii. Honolulu: Hawaii Hiroshima Heritage Study Group, 2001.

Harby, Bill. "Hands On." *Island Scene*. December 1999. http://www.islandscene.com/ohana/1999/991202/hands_on/.

Hawai'i Department of Land and Natural Resources website: http://www.state.hi.us/dlnr/dsp/oahu.html

"Hawaii Skatepark Progress Page." http://www.50-50.com/absorb/articles/2001/skatepark_progress.shtml

James, Van. *Ancient Sites of Oahu.* Honolulu: Bishop Museum Press, 1991.

Juvik, James O., et al. *Student Atlas of Hawaii.* Honolulu: Bess Press, 2000.

Kam, Nadine. "The Weekly Eater: Ronnie's bringing families back to the table." *Honolulu Star-Bulletin.* April 14, 2002.

Lo, Catherine. "Attn: girls who want to rip." *Honolulu Weekly.* January 29, 2003.

Masuoka, Brandon. "Just about anyone can learn." *Island Weekly.* January 30, 2003.

McMahon, Richard. *Camping Hawaii: A Complete Guide.* Honolulu: University of Hawai'i Press, 1997.

Mitchell, Donald Dean. *Hawaiian Games for Today.* Honolulu: Kamehameha Schools Press, 1975.

Pukui, Mary Kawena, et al. *Place Names of Hawaii.* Honolulu: University of Hawai'i Press, 1989.

Schmitt, Robert C. *Firsts and Almost Firsts in Hawai'i.* Honolulu: University of Hawai'i Press, 1995.

Schmitt, Robert C. *Hawaii Data Book.* Honolulu: Mutual Publishing, 2002.

"Summer Stuff 2003." *Island Family.* Honolulu, Hawaii. March 2003.

"Tiny Tot Program." *The Teddy Bear Post: A Newsletter for Parents of Preschoolers,* vol. 7, no. 7. Spring 2003.

Tsai, Michael. "Skateboarding kicks into mainstream." *Honolulu Advertiser.* August 18, 2002.

"Walking Tour of Historic Downtown Honolulu." http://www.alohafriends. com/historichonolulu.html

Walters, William. *Short Bike Rides Hawaii.* Guilford, Conn: Globe Pequot Press, 1998.

Westervelt, William D. Hawaiian. *Legends of Old Honolulu.* Tokyo: Charles E. Tuttle Company, 1963.

Williamson, Susan. *Summer Fun! 60 Activities for a Kid-Perfect Summer.* Charlotte, Vt: Williamson Publishing, 1999.

INDEX

About the Author

Carrie Ching was born and raised in Kailua. As a keiki she surfed, hiked, biked, and camped all over the island. Now she takes her nephews exploring on new adventures around Oʻahu. She is a freelance journalist and co-author of *A Pocket Guide to Diamond Head and Waikīkī.*

About the Illustrator

Lance Bowen lives on Maui where he relocated with his wife from Southern California. After his first visit to the islands in 1962, he was hooked on Hawaiʻi's warm air, warm water, and warm aloha spirit. As a freelance illustrator and cartoonist, Bowen still has fun drawing when he's not out surfing Maui's westside waves.